HOME AND DISTANT

HOME AND DISTANT

A 40-year railway career from apprentice fitter to BRB headquarters, 1952-93

Brian Grant

· W O R K I N G   L I V E S ·
from
The NOSTALGIA Collection

ACKNOWLEDGEMENTS

First of all I would like to thank all my friends and railway colleagues for the help and inspiration they gave to me throughout my railway career. In particular I would like to thank the following people who were instrumental in helping me in my chosen career: Fred Hales, Claude Dare, John Rodgers, Fred Brookes, David Pattisson, Charles Coxon, Grant Woodruff, Claude Hankins and Roy Calvert.

In addition, my thanks go to the following for supplying photographs: The Southern Railway, Waterloo, Salisbury Times, British Railways and British Rail Western Region, L. Elsey, Southern Newspapers Ltd, Middlesex County Times, Reading Evening Post and Will Adams.

Finally my thanks to Geoff Body for his help and useful comments, which enabled me to produce this book.

To Thelma, Lyn, Kay, Mark and Zoe

A Silver Link book
from
The NOSTALGIA *Collection*

© Brian Grant 1998

All rights reserved. No part of this publication may be reproduced, stored in a retrieval system or transmitted, in any form or by any means, electronic, mechanical, photocopying, recording or otherwise, without prior permission in writing from Silver Link Publishing Ltd.

First published in March 1998

British Library Cataloguing in Publication Data

A catalogue record for this book is available from the British Library.

ISBN 1 85794 106 3

Silver Link Publishing Ltd
The Trundle
Ringstead Road
Great Addington
Kettering
Northants
NN14 4BW

Printed and bound in Great Britain

CONTENTS

My grandfather, Driver Mark Grant, gives No 455 *Sir Launcelot* a final check at Waterloo. *Southern Railway*

INTRODUCTION

Like most young boys I was completely fascinated by railways from an early age. This was hardly surprising as my father had been an apprentice fitter on the London & South Western Railway (later incorporated into the Southern Railway), during and after the First World War. Unfortunately, due to the economic situation at the time, his employment, like that of many others, was terminated when his apprenticeship was completed. After a few months of temporary work he joined the Merchant Navy as a Junior Engineer and progressed to the position of Chief Engineer by the time of his retirement in 1965.

The other railway influence on me was that of my paternal grandfather, Mark Grant, who joined the LSWR at Nine Elms in 1890 as an engine cleaner. He transferred to Bournemouth in 1896 as a fireman, then obtained a driver's position at Salisbury in 1904, retiring from the top link there in 1936. His final trip, accompanied by his regular fireman, Harry Yelland, involved working the 3pm service from Waterloo to Salisbury with his own 'King Arthur' Class 4-6-0 locomotive No 455 *Sir Launcelot*.

During the Second World War my grandfather was re-employed by the Southern Railway as a train attendant to ensure that all blinds were drawn on the Salisbury-Waterloo trains allocated to him. How long this lasted I cannot remember, but I do have a memory of him coming home one day with a broken thumb that had been trapped in a sliding door.

My own earliest recollections of the

The layout of Salisbury station.

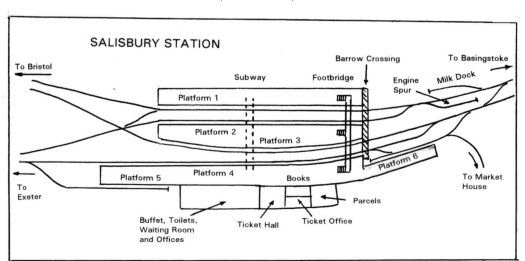

LSWR 4-4-0 No 680 heads the 12.30pm Waterloo to Bournemouth service on 19 August 1901. Driver J. Wilt is at the regulator and his fireman is my grandfather, Mark Grant. *Author's collection*

Southern Railway are from the times I went with my grandfather to the engine sheds or the station at Salisbury to collect his weekly pension, which amounted to the grand sum of 16s 9d. Usually, if we went to the depot, there would be time for a walk round so that grandfather could meet his old colleagues and I could join them on the footplate and listen avidly while they chatted about their past experiences. Visits to the station always included time to watch the locomotives being changed on services to and from Waterloo and those operated jointly by the Southern Railway and the Great Western between the South Coast and Bristol/Cardiff.

Salisbury originally had two stations, a terminus with two platforms used by GWR trains, and a larger six-platform through station built by the LSWR. When the former was closed in 1932 all services were transferred to the larger station where Bristol/Cardiff trains used No 1 platform, West of England services No 2 and those in the reverse direction Nos 3 and 4 respectively. The latter platform incorporated two bays, No 5 for local

services to Yeovil and Exeter and No 6 for trains to Bournemouth, Bulford and Portsmouth. Opposite Platform 6 there was a short loading dock for handling the milk churns on their way to the Express Dairies depot, and a short siding used for locomotives awaiting onward services. Another siding, about 800 yards long, branched off No 6 to serve the Market House near the town centre.

As the war in Europe drew to a close I obtained my first Ian Allan books containing the details of the Southern and Great Western locomotive fleets, and I was soon underlining the numbers of those visiting Salisbury. As the station had through services to Bournemouth, Portsmouth, Exeter, Waterloo, Bristol and Cardiff there was always plenty of variety. On a typical 3-4 hour visit to the station one could expect to see 'Merchant Navy', 'West Country' and 'Battle of Britain' locomotives on the West of England services with locals being hauled by 'H15', 'N15', 'S15' and 'T9' Class engines. A 'Lord Nelson' regularly worked one of the Salisbury-Waterloo locals, and on odd occasions a 'T14' or

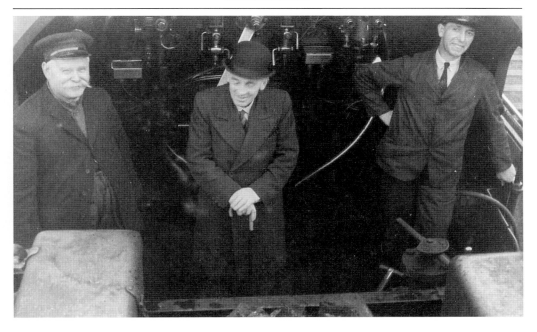

Above At the end of a 46-year career, Driver Grant is pictured on 27 December 1936 with Fireman H. Yelland and Locomotive Superintendent E. S. Moore. They are on the footplate of No 455 *Sir Launcelot* prior to working the 3 o'clock service from Waterloo to Salisbury. *Author's collection*

Below Another photograph of Driver Grant with senior railway officers. *Author's collection*

"KING ARTHUR" OF THE SOUTHERN RAILWAY. 4-6-0. EXPRESS ENGINE No. E.453.

DESIGNED BY MR R. E. L. MAUNSELL, C.B.E. ONE OF THE ENGINES USED IN WORKING THE PRINCIPAL FAST EXPRESSES BETWEEN LONDON (WATERLOO) AND EXETER, AND ALSO THE HEAVY CONTINENTAL BOAT TRAINS BETWEEN LONDON (VICTORIA) AND DOVER.

CYLINDERS	20½ INS. x 28 INS.	LENGTH OVER BUFFERS	64 FT. 8½ INS
DRIVING WHEELS	6 FT. 7 INS.	WEIGHT OF ENGINE & TENDER	129 TONS 1 CWT
BOGIE WHEEL	3 FT. 7 INS.	BOILER PRESSURE	200 LBS. PER SQ. IN

Maunsell's 'King Arthurs' made their debut in 1925. The lower picture shows my grandfather's engine, No 455 *Sir Launcelot*, at Salisbury. This locomotive was one of the first batch. *Both author's collection*

'Remembrance' Class locomotive might appear on a local service.

On the GWR side, while 'King' Class locomotives were not permitted over the routes to Salisbury due to weight restrictions, the trains to Bristol and Cardiff could be hauled by 'Castles', 'Halls', 'Manors', 'Granges', 'Bulldogs' or even a 'Saint'.

SR freight services were usually headed by 'H15', 'S15', 'N1' or 'U1' locomotives, with the local trip to Bournemouth allocated to a member of the '700' Class. Great Western heavy freight services from South Wales were usually powered by a '28XX' or '72XX' locomotive, but on the local trips from Bristol or Westbury the engine class varied from day to day with '43XXs' taking their turn with '56XX' and '57XX' machines.

In 1947 I changed schools, a move that meant not only having to use my bicycle for the school journeys, but more importantly having to pass the station on the way. It was a regular routine to leave home about 8.20am and meet other school friends at the station where we could see which locomotives had worked the first service from Bristol and the local stopping service from Yeovil Junction. Usually these trains were worked by a 'Hall' and an 'N15' Class respectively, and both provided a connection with the Waterloo service, which departed from Salisbury about 8.30. On the way home we made another call to view the local afternoon service from Waterloo and the evening one to Bournemouth. Additional evening and weekend visits made a break from homework, and we also discovered two new vantage points from which it was possible to see locomotives being serviced in the SR engine shed.

At this period Salisbury had two engine sheds, a large one for Southern locomotives and a smaller GWR facility. West of the station the two routes ran parallel for some 3 miles, and one of our new vantage points involved climbing a wall between the bridges that carried the two sets of lines over Cherry Orchard Lane, where the SR shed was situated. On Saturdays and during school holidays this was ideal for spotting any competition between trains on the two routes.

The down 'Atlantic Coast Express' was booked to depart from Salisbury some 10 minutes after a service to Bristol, but if the latter was running late there could often be an exciting race to Wilton where the two routes diverged.

From our vantage point it was possible to look over to the area around the turntable and watch locomotives as they were being moved from the coaling area. It was here, too, that I had my first success with placing a penny on the line to have it flattened by a 'Merchant Navy' Class locomotive. With hindsight I realise the dangerous position we placed ourselves in, being so close to the running lines!

The Great Western shed was situated in a much more open area and our favourite watching spot there was the disused cattle pens, adjacent to the outlet from the shed. It was from here that I obtained my first trip on the footplate of the '97XX' locomotive that was doing the shunting in Fisherton Yard. This yard was the focal point for empty mineral wagons returning to South Wales and had regular trips from Salisbury East and West Yards.

We tried many times to make unauthorised visits to the SR shed. If either Bert Miller or Jack Parker was the duty shed foreman, it was usually possible as they had both been at school with my father and knew me. In their absence we often took a chance by creeping under the window of the timekeeper's office, but only on a few occasions did we manage to see everything in the depot. Usually we would get only part way round before being detected and escorted off the premises!

With a father in the Merchant Navy there were plenty of opportunities to visit him when his ship was in dock in London, Southampton or Avonmouth. I particularly looked forward to the visits to Avonmouth as they entailed a change of trains at Bristol Temple Meads and the possibility of seeing LMS locomotives. While the London and through services used Platforms 1 to 9 of the splendid 1865-78 station, those for the Midlands and North used the original Brunel terminus of 1840. Among the kaleidoscope of Bristol memories is one of a Midlands train headed by 'Jubilee' Class 4-6-0

No 45696 *Arethusa*. A passenger asked the guard a question just after he had given 'right away', and by the time the poor chap had answered, his train was on the move and he could only watch it disappear into the distance!

In 1950 opportunities arose to spread my areas of trainspotting. Visits were made to Eastleigh and Swindon Locomotive Works on the Open Days, and the sight of the skill that went into the manufacture and maintenance of the locomotives there had a great influence on my eventual choice of career. In addition, as my brother was doing his National Service at Lydd, a friend and I would meet him at Waterloo and visit some of the other major London stations. At Euston and King's Cross I saw my first 'foreign' 'Pacific' locomotives. While the 'Princess' and 'Coronation' Classes appeared to exude power, it was the LNER streamlined 'A4s' that really took my eye.

With such an interest in railways it was only natural, when the time came for me to consider what to do when I left school, to look for employment on the railway, although many of my friends did not consider this to be appropriate for someone who had attended a Grammar School! Accordingly, the first steps in my chosen career were taken in August 1952 when my father accompanied me to the locomotive depot in Cherry Orchard Lane. I was interviewed by the shedmaster, Mr Hales, and filled in the necessary application form. Following a medical examination at Eastleigh Works I was accepted for an apprenticeship and told to report for work on 1 September. Never having had a job before I was a bit apprehensive about what lay ahead, but at least I knew something of the Salisbury engine shed and many of the staff I would work with there.

1
SALISBURY APPRENTICESHIP

Salisbury engine sheds, located some 800 yards west of the station, consisted of a single-ended building and ten sidings, of which eight could hold four main-line locomotives. Numbers 1 and 2 roads were used for locomotives undergoing boiler-washing and the routine examinations associated with this work, while No 3 road was usually reserved for locomotives awaiting repairs or mileage examinations and No 4 for the breakdown train, which was made up of a 36-ton steam crane with tool and mess vans.

While roads 5 to 9 were in general use for stabling locomotives awaiting subsequent services, it was normal practice for those undergoing mileage examinations to be placed at the dead-end of these lines. The depot's independent snow plough was placed at the dead-end of No 8 road, as was its later replacement, which was used with a '700' Class goods engine.

No 9 road was fitted with an overhead platform for working on the top of boilers, while two 40-ton glw electric hoists, one fixed and the other mobile, were located in No 10; these could be used to lift any locomotive that required the removal of wheels or bogies. Although the gross weight of the 4-6-2 'Pacific' engines exceeded 80 tons, it was permissible to lift them provided a set of wheels or bogie was left on the rails to reduce the total weight.

Water columns were provided outside the depot, while inside each road was fitted with a number of low-voltage electrical supply points and connections to the depot compressed air system. In addition, 400-volt electrical points were provided at various places in the shed for the electric welding apparatus.

On the north side of the shed area were the coaling facilities, consisting of two separate lines on either side of the coal stage. Coaling of locomotives was carried out either by using a conveyor belt on the south side of the stage or by means of 'tubs' on the north side. Both coaling lines gave access to the turntable and a single line led from there to the rest of the depot. Coal wagons awaiting placement were stabled in a siding adjacent to the down main line to Exeter. A coal stacking area was located at the east end of Nos 1 and 2 roads.

Between the coal stage and the depot there was a single siding where stores vans were unloaded. A regular fortnightly service operated between Salisbury and Eastleigh Locomotive Works to ensure that components requiring overhaul or replacement were dealt with expeditiously. Also, in the event of a failure of the compressed air supply a Westinghouse-fitted locomotive could be placed at the end of this siding and coupled to the depot's system.

Salisbury's locomotive stores were housed below the depot water storage tank and adjacent to the turntable, toilets and washrooms.

Staff who worked in the depot during the Second World War would recount the story of one of the rare visits by enemy aircraft, when the station and sheds were strafed with cannon fire. A bomb was also dropped but failed to explode, although it struck the track at the depot entrance, passed through the coaling plant amid a cloud of coal dust, severed a water pipe and finished up in the allotments on the

Above 'S15' Class locomotive No 30834 on the turntable at Salisbury loco depot. *Salisbury Times*

Southern Region steam: an SR 'Pacific' at work on the 7.15pm Salisbury to Waterloo, seen passing Porton on 28 June 1959 (*below left*); 'Schools' Class No 30911 *Dover* at Broken Cross Bridge (*below right*); and (*opposite*) a strange locomotive combination at Eastleigh. *Author's collection*

other side of Cherry Orchard Lane. The offices, messrooms and sand-drying rooms were near the dead-ends of the sidings. Notice cases, with details of footplate staff rosters, general and 'Late Notices' seemed to occupy most of the space on the walls outside the offices and messrooms, the maintenance staff having their own private collection of notices for some reason. On the wall outside the timekeeper's office a further notice board gave details of the locomotives allocated to various trains and those under or awaiting repairs or examinations.

The role of Salisbury shed was to provide engines and men to work the area's train services, and all these facilities existed to that end. The locomotive maintenance activity entailed both emergency repair and routine maintenance, the latter based on examinations fixed by the length of time in traffic or the mileage run. Linked with boiler-washing, for example, were renewal of the gauge glasses used to indicate the level of water in the boiler, cleaning the injectors used to maintain that level, cleaning the cones in the vacuum ejector for the braking system, refacing back pressure valves and packing the glands on steam valves. There were also six mileage examinations carried out at frequencies of 5-6,000 miles; the odd-numbered ones were mainly concerned with visual and physical examination of the

locomotive's motion (coupling rods and valve gear) and checking the wear on locomotive tyres, while the even-numbered ones were more detailed and culminated in the removal of valves and pistons at No 6.

A shedmaster had overall responsibility for the efficient running of the location, with support on the operating side from a senior running foreman, and with a foreman fitter for maintenance matters. A chief clerk dealt with 'staff' matters, and individual clerks were responsible for rosters, timesheets, paybills, stores and stationery. Shed staff had to book on and off with the timekeeper for each shift.

The foreman fitter had a non-clerical assistant who looked after locomotive records, prepared examination cards and kept the paperwork in order. An apprentice usually got this job if the regular incumbent was not available, and I always welcomed this as a good opportunity to absorb information and widen my knowledge.

All locations like Salisbury had their own allocation of diagrams showing the work to be undertaken by men and machines. The duty running foreman was responsible for allocating the correct class of locomotive to each diagram, and although the roster clerk performed this function for footplate staff, the running foreman had to cover the manning of specials such as the breakdown train, often at short notice.

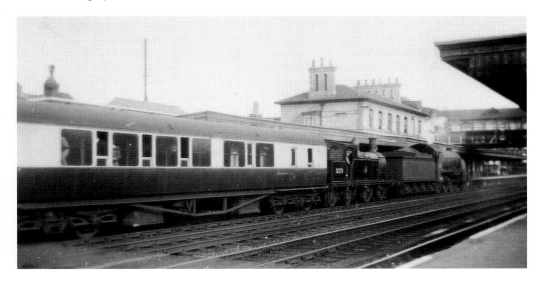

During the period that I worked in the sheds at Salisbury the complement of allocated locomotives varied between 65 and 70. Included in this total were three 'Merchant Navy' and eight or nine 'West Country'/'Battle of Britain' Class locomotives. These were normally allocated to the main-line services, with local services to Bournemouth and Portsmouth usually entrusted to 'T9' Class engines – although I do recall occasions when an 'M7' tank or a 'West County' or 'Battle of Britain' locomotive was rostered on a Bournemouth service.

In normal times the 'N15', 'H15' and 'S15' locomotives were usually allocated to local services to Yeovil and to a variety of freight and civil engineering services, many of which involved trains to and from Meldon Quarry, near Okehampton. In emergencies and during the peak summer holiday period main-line passenger trains were often worked by members of those three classes, with the additional services to Weymouth and Swanage hauled by 'West Country' or 'Battle of Britain' locomotives. At the other end of the locomotive hierarchy, the Salisbury station pilot was usually an 'M7', with the shunting of Fisherton and East Yards covered by a '97XX' or 'G6' and 'Z' Class locomotives respectively.

I will always remember Monday 1 September 1952. On that damp and miserable day I made my first journey to the engine sheds in Cherry Orchard Lane to begin at 7.30am an apprenticeship covering the repair and maintenance of steam locomotives. I had been accepted for a job I was sure would be interesting, but I was still apprehensive about what the future had in store and could never have foreseen where it would eventually lead me.

The apprenticeship would be divided into three sections and would end when I reached the age of 21. The first three years were spent in Salisbury engine sheds, and this was followed by one year in Eastleigh Locomotive Works. At the end of the Eastleigh period I returned to Salisbury for a final year as an 'improver' and was then allowed to work on my own, albeit under partial supervision.

After reporting to the time office I was introduced to Phillip Broom, one of the two leading fitters, who gave me a brief explanation of the work undertaken at the depot. It did not make a lot of sense to me at the time, but I was soon to realise that the range of repairs and examinations was wide, right up to the No 6 examination carried out when a locomotive had accumulated between 30,000 and 36,000 running miles.

The Salisbury maintenance staff at the time included five fitters and their assistants working on shifts and only dealing with running repairs to locomotives in service. Three Category 2 fitters, also on shifts, dealt with such things as brake adjustments and other minor service repairs. Fitter Joe Beale and his assistant, Bill Gale, were allocated to locomotives undergoing boiler-washing.

Although three fitters and assistants were responsible for major examinations and repairs that could not be encompassed by the staff working shifts, most of my first two years was with fitter Basil Norris and his assistant, Toby Downer. All fitters could deal with examinations and repairs, but these two spent most of their time on major examinations. Three boilersmith and assistant pairs did the work on locomotive boilers, with two ancillary staff responsible for cleaning fireboxes and renewing brick arches (the latter were located in the firebox and served two basic purposes, to ensure the heat from the fire circulated before being drawn through the boiler tubes, and to reduce the effect of extreme heat on the tube ends).

The shedmaster had overall responsibility for the depot with assistance from a foreman fitter in charge of the maintenance staff. The shift running foremen supervised the 'conciliation' staff, most of whom worked a day shift and were responsible for keeping the shed tidy, boiler-washing duties and the provision of oil in certain types of axleboxes on bogies and locomotive tenders. The coal stage was staffed on all shifts.

I was only the second apprentice at Salisbury and, after the initial period with Basil Norris, I worked with other fitters on specific jobs, quickly appreciating the variety of the work and the opportunity to acquire knowledge and experience. Although the work was heavy and dirty at times, I rarely wondered whether I should have pursued my other career prospect as a Physical Training Instructor.

Among friendly and helpful colleagues I could not have wished for a better start to my apprenticeship. The first three years literally flew by, and I was then faced with the prospect of a year at Eastleigh Locomotive Works. Never having been away from home before, I was again a bit apprehensive, especially as it was not possible to commute and I would have to find lodgings at Eastleigh.

Fortunately the other apprentice from Salisbury, who was two years ahead of me, had found an excellent place that was not on the official list. I made this my first call, and Mrs Davis said that she would take me if nothing else was available. I dutifully tried the recommended places but, fortunately, none could help so I took up residence with the Davis family in Goldsmith Road. It proved a home from home and I acquired a sister, spending some pleasant times with Yvonne Davis and enjoying technical discussions with her father who worked in the railway brass foundry.

Eastleigh Locomotive Works was divided into a number of 'shops' where the complete overhaul of locomotives and their components was carried out. Initially all locomotives in for general repairs were completely stripped and the individual parts despatched to the appropriate shops for renovation or renewal. Eventually all the components were returned to the Erecting Shop where the locomotive was re-assembled, then taken to the weighbridge to ensure that the weight distribution on each wheel met the design specification. This was followed by transfer to Eastleigh shed and allocation to a booked service, before the engine returned to its home depot. One of these trial services involved an early morning freight working to Salisbury and back.

Unfortunately I only got to work in the Brass and Fitting Shops, and compared with the variety of work I had been involved with at Salisbury, I found the 12 months at Eastleigh rather boring. My father had served part of his apprenticeship there and I found it

strange that, some 40 years later, people like Harry Pemberton were still doing the job they had done in my father's time.

I also noticed a significant disparity in earnings between the staff in Salisbury sheds and those in Eastleigh Works. The former were expected to carry out a wide variety of tasks, many of them on locomotives 'in steam', and this was recognised by a bonus payment of 27.5 per cent. However, in the Works bonus payments could be as high as 130 per cent, and this for doing similar work all the time. I came to suspect some bad 'time measurements', but it was also rumoured that the level of output was manipulated to achieve the highest possible bonus.

The difference between working in the two situations was highlighted by an incident that occurred during my Eastleigh stay. A locomotive 'on trial' from the local sheds developed a leaking gland on a steam valve and was allocated to a fitter who had never worked on an engine in steam before. He proceeded in his normal manner without taking any account of a boiler pressure in excess of 200 lbs per sq in (psi), and was lucky to escape injury when this pressure shot the gland nut out of the steam valve.

The three months I spent in the Brass Shop were very enjoyable, and I even played darts for them at the local Railway Institute. To relieve the work monotony we apprentices would challenge one another to see how many 'castle' nuts could be produced in an hour, and managed to push the record up to well over a hundred. There was plenty of overtime available and doing my share meant being able to afford the thick cheese sandwiches available from the canteen.

The impatience of youth led me into a difference of opinion with the foreman concerning gauge glass frame assemblies with removable cocks. After removal from the locomotives these went to the Brass Shop where the agreed procedure was to loosen the nuts holding the cocks and immerse the whole assembly in an acid bath to remove limescale. After washing, the assembly was then returned to the bench for final cleaning, a lengthy refacing of the mating surfaces and repacking of the glands. If a careful check of the mating surfaces revealed no leakage, I felt that coating them with a thin film of oil was sufficient and was soon producing a greater turnover of assemblies than was usual. Summoned to the foreman, I explained my method of operation but, despite there being no evidence of subsequent failure of the units I had overhauled, the traditional method prevailed, ostensibly because it had been used in the time measurements on which the bonus scheme was based.

This was my first encounter with 'time measurement', and it suggested that there were ways to subvert any work study system if those making the assessment did not have the necessary practical work experience. This was further highlighted later in my career when an attempt was made to introduce work study ideas into engine shed work schedules. The team allocated to setting time limits on all the numerous tasks associated with the repair and maintenance of locomotives were woefully short of practical experience. In one instance a team member suggested that it would be quicker to use a file on a case-hardened motion pin rather than take it to a grinding machine!

I spent the final nine months of my Eastleigh year in the Fitting Shop where there was plenty of variety. My duties included the overhaul of all valve gear and connecting and coupling rod components, and I was responsible for fitting bushes and motion pins in the former and bushes in the latter. I also had a spell on the overhaul of mechanical lubricators; these were then a comparatively new innovation, but sight-feed ones had been around for many years and were dealt with in the Brass Shop.

The 4-6-2 'Merchant Navy' Class locomotives had been designed by O. V. S. Bulleid and introduced in 1941 for hauling heavy express passenger trains between London and Bournemouth, Exeter, Dover and Ramsgate. Originally classified '2C1' in accordance with Continental practice, these locomotives incorporated a number of features new to the Southern Railway. These included an oil bath similar to a car sump for the motion, steam-operated firehole doors, a steam-driven electrical generator, multiple-jet

blastpipes, and piston valves operated by rocking gear. There were also rocking firebars and thermic syphons in the firebox (to increase the heating surface), drop grates, mechanical lubricators and an increased boiler pressure of 280 psi. Steel stays replaced copper in the firebox and had a hole drilled through their centre to help in the identification of fractures. The oil baths were prone to serious oil leaks and problems with the chain-operated valve gear, but overall streamlining gave the locomotive a graceful appearance, and led to the nickname 'Spam Cans'.

During my period at Eastleigh work was being carried out on the prototype of a 'modified' 'Merchant Navy' Class locomotive. No 35018 British India Line had been selected, and I had the job of overhauling its mechanical lubricators. The main changes from the original locomotive design included the removal of the oil bath and the streamlining to improve access to the reversing gear, the fitting of conventional Walschaerts valve gear, and mechanical instead of steam-operated reversing gear. In addition, grease replaced oil as the lubrication medium at many points, thus reducing the length of preparation time. Although I was a great advocate of streamlining, the modified 'Merchant Navy' locomotives always looked much more powerful.

An efficient steam engine relies on the correct quantity of air being admitted to the firebox to optimise combustion and eliminate fuel wastage. On earlier locomotive types the firehole door was mechanically operated by the fireman, who opened it before adding coal and closed it when he had finished. On the Bulleid designs fitted with a steam-operated door worked by a foot treadle, the door could be closed after each shovel of coal to give greater control over the air flow. However, theory was not always borne out in practice, for I have seen many instances when the firehole door did not open resulting in the fireman's shovel hitting the door and coal going all over the place! Experience has also shown that, due to the good steaming qualities of these locomotives, many firemen never used the automatic system.

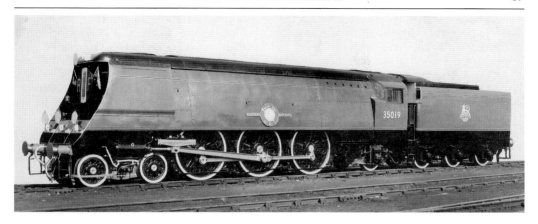

Above 'Merchant Navy' 4-6-2 No 35019 *French Line C.G.T.*, in original form. It carries a headboard showing the emblem of the French Republic on the occasion of a state visit of President Auriol on 3 March 1950. *British Railways*

Below 'Merchant Navy' Class 4-6-2 No 35018 *British India Line* after modification at Eastleigh Locomotive Works. *L. Elsey*

Another factor that inhibits combustion is the build-up of clinker in the firebox, reducing the amount of air being drawn through the fire. On other locomotives firemen had to use a 'dart' to break up the clinker, but on these Bulleid machines the floor of the firebox was fitted with mechanically operated rocking gear, which partially rotated the fire bars, breaking up the clinker and allowing it to fall into the ashpan.

At the end of a steam locomotive's turn of duty it was necessary to clean or completely remove the fire. Again, normally this was carried out by using long-handled shovels and removing the waste material through the firehole door, but these Bulleid locomotives were fitted with a drop grate section, which allowed the waste to be deposited in the ashpan. Similarly, most existing smokeboxes were circular and fitted with a fairly tall, single-jet blastpipe, which funnelled the exhaust steam through the chimney and created a vacuum in the smokebox to draw air through the fire. Removal of ash was difficult, but on the Bulleid locomotives a low-height multiple-jet blastpipe and a flat floor made ash removal much easier.

As the water in the area over which the 'Merchant Navy' Class worked was mainly classified as hard, with a high level of impurities, a French water treatment system (TIA) was fitted. Chemical briquettes were placed in a container on the tender and every time water was taken a calculated amount of chemicals was mixed with it. In addition, the locomotives were fitted with automatic and manual 'blow-down' facilities on the boiler. The automatic system allowed a quantity of boiler water to be discharged when the locomotive was moving, thus ensuring that impurities suspended in it were removed without being allowed to settle. One of the benefits was an increase in the intervals between boiler washouts.

For filling the boiler with water, most existing main-line locomotives had two injectors fitted under the footplate on either side, one operated by live steam and the other by the exhaust steam that would otherwise pass straight to the atmosphere. With the precise control available on the exhaust injector, it could be used from the beginning of a journey to the end without having to alter the setting. When the driver closed the regulator the exhaust injector automatically switched over to live steam operation. The Bulleid locomotives, however, had two 'Monitor' live steam injectors, both under the footplate on the fireman's side. To reduce pipework, the clack valves, through which the water entered the boiler, were also on the fireman's side of the boiler.

Instead of using paraffin oil, Bulleid-designed locomotives had a steam-operated electric generator providing power for the lights at front and rear. In addition, electric lighting was provided in the cab itself to enable the boiler water level to be monitored, the driver to see the position of the steam-operated reversing gear and the fireman to ensure that the injectors were not wasting water.

To eliminate leakage from live steam glands on the piston valves a system of valve operation by means of rocking gear between the piston heads, in the exhaust steam chamber, was adopted. Also, whereas steam valve glands were normally packed with asbestos, on these locomotive pre-formed packing rings were used. Likewise, while piston valve packings were normally made from phosphor bronze, these engines used cast iron rings.

A critical feature in the safe operation of a steam boiler was the ability to identify the level of water within it. If it fell too low, fusible plugs, incorporated as a safety precaution, would melt, allowing the remaining water to extinguish the fire, but damage would be caused to the firebox. Normally monitoring was by means of two circular gauge glasses, but the Bulleid machines had Klinger gauge frames consisting of reinforced glass in a metal frame. Many, however, thought that these were not an improvement.

On completion of the modification work, the new-look *British India Line* was allocated to a series of test runs between Waterloo and Bournemouth, most of the Eastleigh staff turning out to watch the first one. After many successful runs the decision was taken to modify further 'Merchant Navy' locomotives, and subsequently the 'West Country' and 'Battle of Britain' Classes.

As I approached the end of my period in the locomotive works I tried to get permission to complete my apprenticeship there, but this was refused and in July 1956 back I went to Salisbury. I was still classified as an apprentice, but the increased variety of work was welcome and I did get some jobs to do on my own. There did seem to be a lot of dirty jobs, such as changing superheater elements – perhaps this was part of the learning curve – but these were usually compensated by opportunities to work on repairs and examinations with a fitter and his mate.

As explained earlier, examinations on steam locomotives were based on either time in service or on the mileage run, culminating in the No 6 examination. This included the removal of all valves and pistons and, in most cases, the fitting of new cast iron rings. On locomotives with sight-feed lubricators the removal of piston valves could be a very difficult task as carbon, created by burnt oil, tended to accumulate under the cast iron rings fitted on the valve heads. On many occasions

I found it necessary to use a hydraulic jack to force the valve through the valve liner, and on one occasion it was even necessary to break the valve heads.

To overcome this problem I learned one of the tricks of the trade practised by experienced fitters. It involved filling the lubricator with paraffin about a week before the locomotive was due to be 'stopped' for examination. The paraffin tended to soften the carbon and make it easier to remove the piston valves and the carbon build-up in the steam passages. The Bulleid locomotives did not have this problem as their mechanical lubricators supplied plenty of oil, which did not burn, and it was quite a simple task to remove the valves and pistons. In some cases I found that removal and cleaning was sufficient, with no need to replace the cast iron rings.

On many locomotives the white metal bushes on the coupling and connecting rods had to be re-metalled at the No 6 examination, but the benefits of the oil bath on the Bulleid locomotives showed up strongly in reduced wear on the motion. Larger engine sheds had specialist machine operators or coppersmiths, but at Salisbury all the fitters were capable of carrying out ancillary duties. If a bush required re-metalling and machining, the fitter carrying out the examination was responsible for both tasks.

During the No 6 it was also necessary to separate the locomotive from its tender to check for wear on the rubbing plates and intermediate buffing gear and on its springs. Some old engines, such as the 'T9' and '700' Classes, were connected to their tenders by a steel bar with a pin hole in each end, and parting the two was a simple task achieved by compressing the machine under examination between two others. On later locomotives one end of the steel bar was replaced by a threaded section and a nut, which had to be undone with a ratchet spanner. This required considerable effort, achieved by attaching a rope to the end of the spanner and having a number of people haul on it. Whenever you heard the call 'on the rope' you knew what was required!

Another important task was to check that the pipes supplying oil to the axleboxes were clear and undamaged. If a blocked pipe was found it had to be removed from the locomotive and heated in a fire to anneal it and remove any blockages. Once again the versatility of the staff came into effect as most could use oxy-acetylene equipment to repair a broken pipe.

The breakdown train added to the variety of work at Salisbury. It was usually manned by a fitter, a crane driver and three or four fitter's assistants. Apprentices were not normally allowed to go out of the depot, but I did manage a couple of trips to minor derailments in local yards. Salisbury's train, complete with 36-ton steam crane, covered quite a large area including the routes to such places as Basingstoke, Yeovil, Bournemouth, Westbury, Weymouth and Ludgershall. If two cranes were required it could work in tandem with the cranes from Nine Elms, Exeter or Eastleigh. There will be more on this subject in the next chapter.

We always seemed to be busy at Salisbury sheds and the time never dragged. Almost before I realised it the end of my apprenticeship was approaching. I had no idea what would happen then, as I knew of no vacancies for fitters in the depot even though the apprentice before me had been retained as a Category 1 fitter. However, a few days before my 21st birthday I received a letter to say that I too would be employed at Salisbury in this category from 1 July 1957.

2
WORK AND RESPONSIBILITY

I was at Salisbury from July 1957 until August 1961, and although much of the work there was repetitive – an examination on a tank locomotive is very similar to one on a main-line machine – the one-off jobs were much more interesting. Some of these are described here.

As I had no intention of remaining a Category 1 fitter for the rest of my life, I knew that I had to increase my knowledge and experience and prove my ability in the next few years. Initially I worked on the same type of task that I had handled as an apprentice, but when I was asked to cover a vacancy on the shift repair team I jumped at the opportunity. I had already studied for my Higher National Certificate in Mechanical Engineering and, since steam operation would clearly not last for many more years, I now enrolled, along with Phillip Broom, one of the leading fitters, for a Practical Diesel Engineering Course at the local Technical College. Perhaps this prompted the interest I developed in photography during the Salisbury period.

Although I returned to my original post when the fitter I was replacing returned to work, I was subsequently appointed to another vacancy as the fitter responsible for repairs in No 10 road where locomotives were lifted. Normally the lift was achieved by using two cranes, but when it was necessary to lift a second locomotive before work on the first had been completed, timber blocks were placed under the buffer beam of the second locomotive and the mobile crane used to lift the opposite end. While this was fairly routine work, difficulties could arise and two such instances remain firmly in my mind.

'S15' Class 4-6-0 No 30828 had suffered a broken right-hand centre driving wheel axlebox while working a freight service from Exeter. The locomotive was taken off its train at Dinton and eventually hauled to Salisbury, where it was placed in No 10 road. There it became my responsibility to arrange the lift and remove the driving wheels.

Preparation for lifting was quite an onerous task. Initially the locomotive had to be parted from its tender, a section of the cab roof removed and the boiler emptied to reduce the weight to be lifted. The crippled machine was then positioned under the two electric hoists with a pair of hooks under the front buffer beam and another pair under the main frame below the footplate. If only a bogie was to be removed it was a simple task to remove the bogie securing pin and lift the locomotive to leave the bogie on the track.

In the case of No 30828, which required the removal of the centre driving wheels, it was necessary to remove the coupling and connecting rods, certain sections of the brake gear, the exhaust steam pipe to the injector and the springs and hornstays on the wheel set concerned. After all this the locomotive was ready for lifting but, to my astonishment, the centre driving wheels rose with the locomotive.

Examination revealed that the broken axlebox had spread and become jammed in the axlebox guides. As the locomotive was still only about 3 inches above the track we tried to force the broken axle box downwards with a large bar, but this had no effect whatsoever. The next option was to lower the locomotive, secure the wheels to the track and

Photographs of steam in the Salisbury area: an ex-GWR tank locomotive hauling a very mixed freight train at Wishford (*above left*); a passenger service approaching Salisbury Tunnel behind a BR Standard 4-6-0 locomotive (*above right*); and (*below*) 'Britannia' 4-6-2 No 70004 exciting a lot of interest on a visit to Salisbury. *Author*

try again. Still the broken axlebox did not move, although the track did, rising with the locomotive!

In the end, two of us had to get beneath the raised locomotive and hit the broken axlebox with 14lb hammers until eventually the wheel set dropped. At last the locomotive could be raised well clear and the wheels rolled out from under it.

To prevent distortion of the main frames, locomotives were never left suspended by the cranes for longer than necessary, so No 30828 was lowered back on to the track, its centre horn stays replaced, timber packing put in position and the crane hooks released. The broken axlebox was despatched to Eastleigh Works, together with measurements of the journal diameter and the distance between the axlebox guides, to enable them to manufacture a replacement. The defective axlebox went to the Brass Shop foundry where it could be melted down and used in another casting.

The number of locomotives of each class allocated to a depot was determined by the train working and shunting duties for which that depot was responsible and included an allowance for locomotives undergoing maintenance and examinations and the provision of power for special workings. When it became necessary to alter these allocations, due to amended train workings, the District Motive Power Office would issue a revised allocation. If this meant the transfer of a locomotive from one depot to another, you could be sure that the 'losing' shed would chose an engine in poor condition, probably one that had covered a high mileage or was in need of major repairs.

This appeared to be the case with 'West Country' No 34027 *Taw Valley* when it arrived at Salisbury. After being in service for a few days drivers began complaining that it always seemed short of steam, irrespective of the type of work to which it was allocated. In these circumstances the normal procedure was to check visually for water leaks in the smokebox or firebox, have the boiler washed out, then thoroughly clean all smoke and superheater tubes, the ashpan and tubeplate. A further check was made to ensure that air was not being drawn into the smokebox and thus reducing the draught on the fire and impairing combustion. The locomotive was then returned to service.

Within a very short time there were more 'short of steam' complaints and it was decided to carry out a complete water test.

This involved removing the fire, cooling down the boiler, then completely filling the boiler with water and allowing it to pass through the regulator into the superheater elements and steam pipes and into the steam chest. This test, which I have also used to identify defective superheater elements, should reveal any leaks by escaping water. None were found on No 34027 and the locomotive was again returned to service.

Still the complaints continued, and when *Taw Valley* was working on passenger services she was losing time badly. Something just had to be done. The locomotive was stopped and the task of identifying the problem handed to me. I was aware of the previous tests and saw no point in repeating them, turning instead to other possible causes. Poor-quality coal might be a cause, but other locomotives using the same coal had not suffered. Similarly, as the complaints came from many different drivers I saw no point in discussing the merits of their firemen.

I decided that the problem could be associated with the lack of efficient combustion. The firebox had been completely cleaned three times since the original complaints, so I decide to examine the smokebox thoroughly. After satisfying myself that there was no possibility of air entering it, I turned my attention to the chimney. Under normal circumstances, with a correctly set-up blastpipe, one would expect to find the inside of the chimney completely cleaned by the exhaust steam passing through it, but on this locomotive there was a build-up of carbon.

As the carbon deposits were all around the chimney I suspected that the alignment of the blastpipe was incorrect. Had this happened on a locomotive with a single-jet blastpipe the normal, although unauthorised, practice would have been to fit a metal rod, known as a 'jimmy', across the blastpipe to spread the steam. On a locomotive with a multiple-jet blastpipe this procedure was not possible.

After discussing my ideas with the foreman fitter, we arranged to check the blastpipe measurements on No 34027 with other locomotives in the same class. All tallied except for the diameter of the holes in the top of the pipe. Those on *Taw Valley* were .125 inch less than the others of the class. We now had to remove the blastpipe and either send it to Eastleigh for machining or do the job ourselves. We chose the latter, and although

Preserved 'West Country' Class 4-6-2 No 34027 *Taw Valley* at Didcot. *Author*

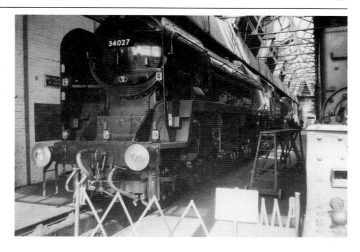

this was not the easiest task in a lathe, it was successful. The machined blastpipe was put back and the locomotive returned to service. No further complaints arose and, as No 34027 has since been preserved, I often wonder how it performs now.

Steel wheels running on steel rails do not provide a locomotive with the best grip under certain climatic conditions. To overcome this, sanding gear is used to increase the friction between the two steel surfaces. The system can vary from gravity-fed dry sand to a steam or water pressure supply, but the objective is basically the same. Whatever the supply system it has to work effectively or disastrous results can arise, as the following example demonstrates.

One of the Salisbury-based 'T9' Class 4-4-0 locomotives, No 30301, was working a late morning service from Bournemouth to Salisbury in damp conditions. The load was only three coaches, a weight of approximately 100 tons, but on leaving Fordingbridge, one of the crossing places on the single line, the wheels slipped on the greasy rails. Then, instead of easing the regulator before operating the sand gear, the driver must have used it while the wheels were still spinning. Unfortunately the sand box on one side of the locomotive was empty, so while the driving wheels on one side were getting a better grip there was no effect on the other. This imbalance subjected the centre driving axle to very high forces with the result that the wheel

that was being restrained by the frictional effect of the sand moved on the axle.

It was fortunate that the incident happened at a passing point on a single line. Although No 30301 could not move under its own power, arrangements were made for another locomotive to place the crippled machine in a siding, then work its train on to Salisbury. I went out with the breakdown train later on the same day; after lifting the locomotive, its defective wheelset was removed, loaded into a wagon and sent to Eastleigh Works. Some weeks later a new wheelset arrived and the process was reversed.

The importance of ensuring that 'foreign' materials do not get into steam pipes is highlighted by an incident involving 'T9' Class 4-4-0 No 30702, which, at a routine boiler examination, was found to have some broken firebox stays. The only way of removing these was to drill the two sections out. While removal of the section in the inner firebox was fairly straightforward, to obtain access to the outer section entailed removal of the injector steam pipes between the steam cocks and the side frame and complete removal of the lagging that covers the firebox. Although the steam pipe unions on the side frames were covered, it appears that during drilling operations some swarf found its way into the steam pipes. After the remedial work was completed a successful steam test was carried out and the locomotive returned to traffic.

'T9' Class locomotive No 30301 standing in a siding at Fordingbridge minus its defective wheelset and showing the tender coupling gear. *Author*

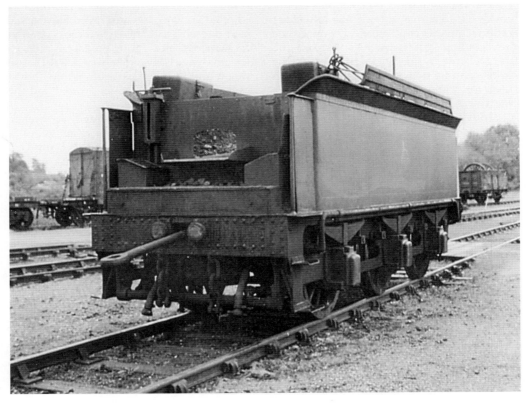

On its first trip the locomotive failed when the crew could not get either injector to work. The fireman had to drop the fire and the locomotive was hauled back to the depot and the offending injectors removed. They revealed no obvious faults but the cones were cleaned in an acid bath to remove any scale. The clearances between the individual parts were checked and found to be within tolerance and, in a subsequent steam test, both injectors worked perfectly.

On its next trip the locomotive failed again, with the original problem. In trying to identify the cause after the second failure both injectors were changed, and when they were removed some copper swarf from the original drilling was found in both steam pipes. After its removal and a further steam test there were no more problems. Again, as with No 34027, it was a question of seeking abnormal causes rather than carrying out routine tasks.

Although I had managed to attend a few derailments during my apprenticeship, I badly wanted to gain more experience by becoming a regular member of the breakdown gang. There was also the extra benefit of overtime, for the crane was regularly used at weekends.

Eventually I got my wish and my name was included among those to be called out. During my last three years at Salisbury I was called out many times, mostly to minor incidents of wagons derailed during shunting operations, but there were also some more serious derailments.

One afternoon we heard that the single line between Downton and Fordingbridge was blocked by a combine harvester and a crane was needed to remove it. On the surface this looked like a simple lifting job, but things turned out to be quite different. After arriving at Downton we left the train and walked along the track to the site of the incident, which was in a cutting at the mouth of a tunnel. We arrived to find just a tangled mass of metal that, two hours earlier, had been a 'combine'. It seemed that this had been at work in the field above the tunnel when the operator felt that something was not quite right. He stopped cutting corn and got down to look beneath the machine. Unfortunately he had left the engine running and while he was underneath the combine it began to move

The Salisbury breakdown crew. Left to right: Basil Norris, Arthur Moore, myself, Tom Stoodley and Arthur Sampson. *Author's collection*

Above Salisbury MPD's breakdown crane in action. *Author's collection*

Left Work completed, the breakdown crew relax over a cup of tea and a game of crib. *Author*

away. Try as he might he could not catch the runaway, and had to watch it push through the fence and fall some 50 feet on to the track. He was very lucky to have escaped injury.

Having assessed the situation we returned to Downton station to arrange to have the breakdown train re-marshalled so that the crane could be propelled to the site. There, the actual work of clearing the track was quite simple. We secured chains on the wrecked combine, lifted it about a foot above the rails and moved back through the cutting. Once clear the wreckage was just lowered into a field at the side of the line.

Another incident involved a partially fitted freight train conveying loaded coal wagons and vans containing milk products from the Cow & Gate depot at Wincanton. On the rising gradient between West Pennard and Evercreech Junction a wagon coupling broke and the brake-van and 16 wagons began to run back down the gradient towards West Pennard station. Although the guard applied the handbrake in his van he could not stop the runaway wagons.

The signalman at West Pennard saw the wagons coming towards his box and managed to divert them into the sidings where they collided with the buffer stops and went in all directions, some finishing up on the single line itself. With hindsight it might have been better to have left the wagons on the running line as the rising gradient towards Glastonbury would have reduced their momentum, but the signalman could not be criticised for applying the rules correctly.

The first priority in any derailment is to clear the running lines so that a normal service can be resumed as soon as possible. Fortunately this freight train was the last service of the day so we could concentrate on removing those wagons that were obstructing the route. Staff from Cow & Gate had joined us and, as the vans were secured, they unloaded them to see whether any of the contents could be salvaged. Once the wagons had been cleared from the running line the permanent way staff carried out the track repairs needed and the breakdown train returned to Salisbury.

The work of recovering the rest of the derailed wagons took three Sundays. Some of the coal wagons were so far from the tracks that we had to drag them back before lifting. About 100 tons of coal was scattered around the field behind the buffer stops, but this quickly vanished and I imagine sales by the local coal merchant were seriously reduced for a while. On the final Sunday, as we re-railed the last wagons, we found about 40 tins of condensed milk, dented but not punctured.

The Cow & Gate people had already said that they had collected anything likely to be of use to them, so these went in the crane toolbox. As it was almost midnight, when we got back to Salisbury the share-out was put off until the following morning, but when we checked the tool box every tin had disappeared!

My first involvement with a derailment where two cranes were required was at Whitchurch South station, and involved a freight train. The freight was not normally booked to stop at Whitchurch, but on the day in question a special passenger train was heading northwards and the two should have passed at Whitchurch South. Instead the freight failed to stop on the falling gradient and was derailed at the protecting trap points, tipping some of its wagons 40 feet down the embankment and into a field.

As it was impossible to lift these wagons they were sold to a local scrap merchant who cut them up and disposed of them. The locomotive, a BR Standard of the 76XXX series, was eventually lifted by the Eastleigh and Salisbury cranes.

In another derailment involving two cranes we were again working with the Eastleigh crane, this time at St Denys station just north of Southampton. In this case the driver of the 13.00 Cardiff to Brighton had misread his signals, run through the sand drag and finished up with No 34022 *Exmoor* partially buried in the end of the platform. This may have been another case where 'familiarity' caused the derailment as the Brighton train normally had a clear run through the junction at St Denys, but on the day in question a special passenger train from Southampton Docks had been given preference.

The derailment was in an awkward place and it proved impossible to position the two cranes for a lift, so other alternatives had to be considered – jacks and packing, ramps or even the Kelbus gear, which consisted of a series of cables and pulleys. It was eventually decided to remove the tender and haul the locomotive backwards with a 350hp 0-6-0 diesel shunter on to rails laid on their sides. The proximity of the River Itchen led to great difficulty in building bases for the crane outriggers, but eventually a base made of

As these pictures graphically show, No 34022 *Exmoor* poses a real challenge for the breakdown crew in this derailment at St Denys on 13 December 1961. *Southern Newspapers Ltd*

sleepers proved successful and the locomotive was re-railed.

Hurstbourne station near Andover, closed for many years, was the scene of another interesting derailment. A '700' Class 0-6-0 goods engine working a local freight service was positioning wagons in the sidings when it became derailed at the points on the main line. To avoid blocking the down main we decided to re-rail with jacks and packing. However, these engines had coil springs on their driving wheels and in the derailment the spring gear became jammed in the points, making it impossible to raise the locomotive at all. I had to go underneath with oxy-acetylene equipment and cut the spring hanger bolts before we could position the hydraulic jacks and start the re-railing.

The dangers of working beside running lines, especially during darkness, was highlighted in a derailment adjacent to Basingstoke West signal box. Although the derailment was in the sidings, the only way that we could get at the derailed wagons was by positioning the crane on the down slow line. This meant that the rear of the crane cab would foul the down fast line every time we slewed the crane.

Accordingly we arranged with the District Inspector for the down fast to be blocked to traffic when we were working. Things were going quite smoothly when, suddenly, a train was seen approaching from Basingstoke station. By sheer good luck the rear of the crane was clear of the down fast and there was no collision. When the signalman was questioned his only response was that he thought we had finished our work!

While all railway work has to be taken seriously, with safety being of paramount importance, there are always funny incidents and one typical example involved the derailment of a loaded cattle truck in Milford Yard, alongside the Salisbury-Southampton line. To get the wagon re-railed it only needed two pairs of chains passed beneath it and then

A view of the derailment of the 10.55am Paddington to Cardiff train at Slough on 1 May 1959. *Author*

Further scenes of the Slough derailment. *Author*

a lift back on to the rails. One of the fitter's mates agreed to go under the wagon and couple the lifting chains together. Unfortunately while he was underneath one of the cows decided to obey the call of nature and proved the floor of the truck to be a less than a perfect seal. Everyone but the poor victim saw the funny side of the incident, but we changed our minds when he had to travel back to the depot with us!

Working with the steam crane was fascinating, partly because no two incidents were the same. This applied not only to derailments but also to weekend engineering operations where the crane was used to remove old bridge structures and position new ones in their place. I was fortunate to be responsible for the renewal of bridges at Yeovil, Sherborne and Warminster.

The main problem with these engineering operations was that they normally took place during the autumn or winter when the weather was very unpredictable. I spent two weekends renewing a bridge south of Yeovil Town station on the Weymouth line, both involving being away from the depot for more than 24 hours, and in continuous rain. The Yeovil job was carried out in November and involved replacing the old bridge with a precast structure.

The one advantage of these pre-planned operations was the advance information on the weights of individual bridge sections, which enabled decisions to be made on the positioning of the crane prior to arrival at the site. However, this did not always work out in practice, as demonstrated by an incident at Yeovil. We had been given a weight of 12.5 tons for the sections of the new bridge and the crane positioning had been worked out accordingly.

When working with a crane one member of the crew was normally stationed on the opposite side to the load, his main job being to watch that the crane wheels remained on the track. We had just lifted a bridge section from its wagon and were lowering the crane jib to position the section on its foundations when there was a shout from the rear of the crane that the wheels were not in contact with the rails. Although we lowered the section and

tightened the outrigger brackets the same thing happened when we tried another lift. We finally managed the task by re-positioning the crane, but later found out that we had been given an incorrect weight for the section. It was during this job that one of the engineering staff slipped when the new section was being positioned and would have been swept away by the river below if we had not had a safety rope across the waterway for just such an eventuality.

The second bridge I renewed was at Sherborne and, once again, the weather was very wet. We left the depot about 17.30 on the Saturday evening and it was still raining when we returned some 28 hours later. We were only renewing a small bridge over a river but the water level rose very quickly and the staff repointing the brickwork after the old bridge section had been removed were fortunate not to get their feet wet.

My third bridge assignment involved a structure over a small lane on the goods loop at Warminster station. When we arrived we found that the permanent way staff had already removed the rails and the ballast. The bridge deck was of a 'corrugated' section so all we had to do was to burn holes at the four corners and lift it out. When we did this it literally crumbled and folded in half; the rails must have been taking most of the weight of the trains that had passed over the bridge!

Conveying prefabricated huts for permanent way staff was usually one of the shorter weekend crane jobs, but I recall one occasion when this work proved anything but routine. We left the depot on Sunday morning with a locomotive hauling the steam crane and a brake-van and headed for East Yard where we were due to attach three Conflats loaded with the prefabricated concrete huts. Only four people, the crane driver, two assistants and myself, were allocated to the job and we were travelling in the brake-van. Waiting in the reception road at East Yard we heard the sounds of a Western Region locomotive, but no one took much notice until we felt the impact as another train struck our brake-van. We were thrown about but luckily our driver had seen the approaching

The breakdown crane and crew working on the replacement of the bridge at Sherborne. *Author's collection*

freight train and released his brakes so that we were only pushed forward. When questioned, the other driver said that he had not expected to find another train in the reception roads on a Sunday morning. He had not seen our train as the lines curved left and he was on a WR engine where the driver was positioned on the right.

While derailments were the main cause of staff being sent out from Salisbury shed, there was one incident where a locomotive had broken down at Dinton and my assistant and I travelled on the footplate of the replacement locomotive. On arrival at Dinton the failed locomotive was placed in a siding and the train continued its journey behind the second engine.

Examination of the failed locomotive revealed that it had a broken piston head in one cylinder. We proceeded to remove the connecting rods and valve operating gear on the side where the piston head was broken in order to centralise the piston valve and enable the locomotive to be hauled back to Salisbury. When we learned that it would be at least 5 hours before assistance could be provided, I decided to try to work the locomotive back on one cylinder. On two-cylinder locomotives the valve gear is so arranged that whenever a locomotive is at rest it is always possible to move it, albeit at times an initial reverse movement is necessary before the locomotive will go forward. With only one cylinder we had to be very careful to stop the locomotive in a position from which it could be restarted, but we managed it and getting the cripple back to the depot gave me a lot of satisfaction.

In 1958 the East Yard and Fisherton Yard pilots at Salisbury were replaced by diesel shunting locomotives. East Yard 'Z' Class No 30957 was replaced with an English Electric 350hp diesel-electric shunter, and Fisherton Yard's 'G6' pilot No 30276 by a Drewry 204hp diesel-mechanical locomotive.

None of the Salisbury shed staff had received diesel maintenance tuition so the locomotives had to be returned to Eastleigh every two weeks; for even a minor fault we had to call for assistance from Eastleigh. To avoid this costly and time-consuming arrangement it was decided that a fitter should be sent on a diesel maintenance course. At the time promotions and matters such as going on courses were normally decided on seniority and, as I was the junior fitter at the depot, I thought it would be months before I got any diesel training. Happily I was wrong, as none of the other fitters wanted to be away from home for several weeks.

I duly commenced a three-month basic training course at Selhurst Training School in January 1959. This was followed by specialist training at various locations – Deptford for Stones boilers, CAV fuel injection equipment at Acton, control equipment at BTH Rugby, Oerlikon brake equipment at Davis & Metcalfe at Manchester, traction motors and generators at Metro-Vickers in Sheffield, and the Sulzer diesel engine at Vickers in Barrow. On completion of the training I returned to Salisbury to find that the diesel scenario was already moving forward, with the introduction of diesel-electric multiple units on services between Salisbury and Portsmouth.

During the period at Selhurst I travelled daily from Salisbury to Waterloo, where I had to catch a local train to Clapham Junction and connect with a train from Victoria to Selhurst. This meant leaving Salisbury at 6.45am and arriving back at 7.06pm, on the 5.00pm from Waterloo. Both the main-line services were worked by top link crews from my home depot.

I have always adopted the practice of checking which locomotive was on any train I used, and during the three months I was at Selhurst I made many footplate trips. Strictly speaking this was only permitted to holders of a footplate permit, but I found that drivers welcomed the professional experience of having a fitter with them to discuss technical issues. There was always the excuse that I was monitoring the performance of the locomotive, but I only had to use this once.

The occasion was early in January 1959 when I was riding on the footplate of 'Battle of Britain' 'Pacific' No 34052 *Lord Dowding* working the 6.45am from Salisbury to Waterloo. The train was booked to call at all stations to Basingstoke, then Woking and Waterloo. We left on time but on arrival at

Above One of my later footplate trips: 'West Country' Class 4-6-2 No 34008 *Padstow* awaits departure from Waterloo in March 1967. *Author*

Below Another footplate trip: this time the train is awaiting departure from Southampton Central. *Author*

Porton the driver was advised that a bank slip had blocked the up line, necessitating single-line working over the down. This system enables trains to run in both directions over a single line, provided of course that they are authorised to do so or accompanied by the pilotman; it was frequently used during weekend track relaying operations. Our pilotman joined us on the footplate and advised the driver that the train had to set back through the crossover, then run on the 'wrong' line to Grateley. This made us about 30 minutes late at Basingstoke, where we were signalled into the fast line platform rather than the slow line one. As we ran into the station the station master saw me and asked Driver Sanger who I was and why I was on the footplate. He used our 'checking the performance of 34052' excuse, which was accepted. Indeed, whenever we met subsequently, the same station master always took a friendly interest in my affairs.

I travelled with most of the top link crews during this period and was able to study their different driving techniques. On one hand there were drivers like Percy Staples and Walt Clissold, who seldom opened the regulator fully and worked the locomotive with a minimum valve cut-off of about 25 per cent. On the other hand there were those, like Bert Cambray and Theo Clissold, who opened the regulator fully as soon as the train was on the move, then quickly reduced the valve cut-off to a very low setting. All these drivers managed to run their trains punctually, but the firemen with the former group had an easier shift and burned considerably less coal.

While we all expect our journeys to be safe and punctual, a number of incidents arose during these Salisbury-Selhurst journeys that showed the sort of problems that can arise.

The 5.00pm service from Waterloo was scheduled to depart from Platform 10 with a set of coaches that had been serviced at Clapham Junction. One Thursday evening No 35013 *Blue Funnel* was working this service and I was on the footplate with Driver Bert Cambray and Fireman George Witt. We departed on time and were approaching the first signal when it suddenly went from green to red. The driver applied the brakes but we could not stop until we had passed the signal. The fireman then went back to the signal to ring the signalman and find out why we had stopped. When he returned he brought the news that the pilot engine that had brought the coaches in from Clapham Junction was still coupled to the rear of the train!

It appeared that when the coaches had arrived in the station the driver of the pilot locomotive had decided to disconnect only the brake pipes, leaving the steam heating pipes coupled to heat the coaches; the coupling was also left in position for removal when the heating pipes were taken off. This must have been forgotten and with no control over the train brakes the pilot was just pulled along by our train locomotive when it set off. Luckily someone had seen what was happening and advised the signalman. After a delay of some 20 minutes we were able to proceed.

On reaching Andover Junction the firemen told the driver than he had changed turns that day in order to take part in a darts match, but he would now be late in reaching the venue. Once the 'right away' was received at Andover, Driver Cambray responded to this challenge and, as we passed Redpost Junction at the start of the climb to Grateley, I sensed that speed was increasing rapidly. A glance at my watch at Grateley station and again as we neared Tunnel Junction signal box at Salisbury brought the realisation that we had covered over 9 miles in 5¼ minutes, an average in excess of 100 mph! One of the things confirmed by this high-speed run was the smooth ride of these 'Merchant Navy' locomotives.

This was not the end of the story as far as No 35013 was concerned. On the following Sunday I arrived for duty at 2.00pm and was confronted by an Exeter driver who was concerned with the noise coming from the big ends of *Blue Funnel*. On examination I found that most of the white metal was missing from both outside big ends, although for some unknown reason the inside big end bearing had not suffered similarly. Obviously the locomotive could not remain in service in this condition, so a replacement was provided and arrangements made for the big ends to be re-metalled and machined on the following day.

Although the overall maximum speed restriction on the line from Waterloo to Salisbury was 85 mph, other instances of excessive speeds have been recorded. The speed of the 'Atlantic Coast Express' was checked by radar apparatus for six days on Enham Bank, on the approach to Andover Junction. On five days speeds above 90 mph were recorded, and on the sixth the speed was over 100 mph!

Driver Bert Cambray seemed to be plagued with problems, one of which occurred on April Fool's Day. Once again I was on the footplate with him on the 6.45am from Salisbury, the locomotive being No 35006 *Peninsular & Oriental S. N. Co.* When we arrived at Andover I was talking to the fireman and we could hear Bert in conversation with the driver of a local service standing on the other side of the island platform.

When the 'right away' signal was given by the station staff, Bert told us that this other driver was trying to play an April Fool's joke on him by insisting that the coupling rods of No 35006 were buckled. Bert clearly had no intention of falling for such a simple ruse, but then had to change his mind as the locomotive started to move and the fireman saw that the rear section of the coupling rod on his side was indeed buckled. A 'T9' Class locomotive was found to haul No 35006 to Andover shed and take the train forward. With its 6 ft 7 in driving wheels, the 'T9' had difficulty starting a heavy train, but once on the move it was capable of quite a reasonable speed. As the 'T9' was the only locomotive available at the time, we had to endure a very erratic journey to Waterloo.

Following the training period at Selhurst I went on to the component factories mentioned earlier. While at Rugby I was able to visit the London Midland Region testing plant where steam locomotives were put through their paces to assess their haulage capabilities. Locomotives were suitably secured on sets of rollers, connected to data measuring equipment, then steamed as if they were in traffic. During my visit a '9F' Class 2-10-0 locomotive was being tested. In a

subsequent discussion with the chief engineer, although he did not know I was a Southern Region man, he mentioned that No 35022 *Holland America Line* was the only locomotive he had tested where full power could not be applied.

Once I had completed the diesel training I began to apply for promotion. I still remember the advice of my shedmaster, Fred Hales: 'Don't expect to get an interview for the first job you apply for or to get the first job you are interviewed for; just persevere and eventually someone will recognise a name that keeps cropping up.' This was to prove very true as I had a number of interviews before I was eventually appointed to a draughtsman's position at Brighton Works. I considered myself fortunate, for such jobs were normally filled from within the office. On the other hand the forward prospects were poor, as there were 36 draughtsmen and only three senior positions, plus the one in charge.

At the time I received notification of my appointment to the job at Brighton I was also notified of an interview for the post of Assistant Mechanical Foreman at King's Cross. The latter had the better prospects so, after a discussion with the shedmaster, I decided to decline the Brighton position and go for the King's Cross interview, despite having no guarantee that I would be selected. As things turned out I was not. However, I was sure other opportunities would come along, and I did have something else to think about as in October 1960 I married Thelma, a girl I had known since school days. She shared my ambitions for promotion and accepted the likelihood of a move, so we started our married life in a rented house belonging to a friend of my parents, in the street where I was born.

I was still keen to widen my knowledge and experience of steam traction, so made regular applications for footplate permits. These resulted in trips to Exeter and from Paddington to Cardiff, and I also took the opportunity to ride on the footplate when I went out with the breakdown train. Additionally, as I was well known to the footplate staff who came to Salisbury, I made many unauthorised trips on services from Salisbury, where drivers were concerned at the

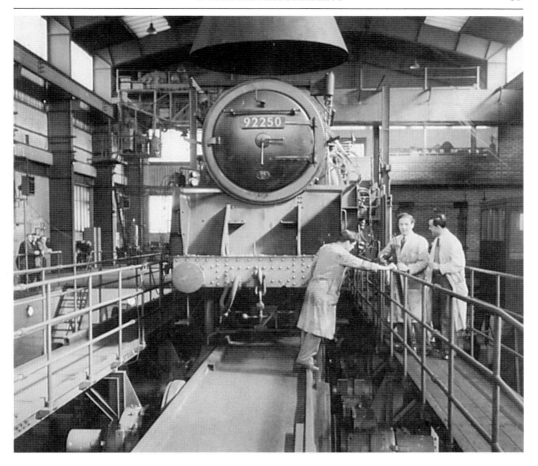

Class '9F' No 92250, numerically the last of its breed, at the Rugby Locomotive Testing Station. *Author*

performance of the locomotive and were looking for a professional opinion. During all these footplate trips only one notable incident occurred, and that was when the fireman had difficulty in raising the water scoop when passing over the water troughs at Fox's Wood and the footplate received a complete wash!

Incidents or not, my knowledge and experience certainly increased. For example, after riding on both modified and unmodified 'Pacifics' I found that the modified locomotives were generally not so free-running, although their steaming qualities were usually better.

In June 1961 I was called for an interview at the Regional HQ at Waterloo in connection with the Motive Power Training Scheme.

This two-year programme gave selected staff training in all aspects of motive power depot operations. I found out at the interview that there were three positions to be filled, one based in each of the SR Divisions. In July I was advised that I had been selected for the one in the South Eastern Division based at Tooley Street, London Bridge. I was told to report at 10.00am on Monday 14 August to commence my training under the direction of the Motive Power Officer.

The last few weeks at Salisbury went very quickly and my last turn as a fitter was the late shift on Sunday 13 August 1961. I believed that I had the necessary technical and practical experience for wider horizons and a good BR future.

3
THE MOTIVE POWER TRAINING SCHEME

On the Monday on which my training began I travelled on the 6.45am train from Salisbury to Waterloo, due to arrive at 9.20. In those days I was so keen that I changed at Basingstoke to the 7.18 from Eastleigh and arrived 20 minutes earlier.

At the London Bridge office I met Jack Morris, chief clerk to the Motive Power Officer, and promptly at 10 o'clock I was called into the latter's office and introduced to Motive Power Officer John Rodgers and Charles Boarer, the shedmaster at Bricklayers Arms. It was explained that my first period of training would take place at Bricklayers Arms and, after a general chat about what was expected of me, I left for 'The Brick' with Charles Boarer. He was the senior shedmaster on the South Eastern Division, recognised as an experienced person with strong leadership qualities, fair to his staff and able to get the best out of them. His main asset was that his staff respected him and they would do all they could for him and Bricklayers Arms.

Charles Boarer's renown was widespread. I was told that on the night of the Lewisham disaster of December 1957 he heard a station broadcast at Charing Cross on his way home, immediately headed for the scene, and on arrival quickly assessed what was required in the way of breakdown trains. There were plenty of other suggestions but no one else was prepared to take on the full responsibility for handling so complex and dramatic an incident, and he stayed on and took overall charge of the recovery work.

While the Lewisham story has been told elsewhere, on a personal note from Bricklayers Arms I heard the story of a driver and fireman who were 'travelling passenger' to Ramsgate on the steam-hauled train. The driver suffered serious leg injuries in the crash, but the fireman was thrown clear and eventually arrived home in a state of shock, unable to recall how he got there.

On arrival at 'The Brick' I was introduced to various people and dealt with the question of accommodation. It was not possible to travel daily from Salisbury, so I had arranged to stay with an aunt and uncle in New Cross. The latter was a driver at Nine Elms and a member of the executive committee of the Associated Society of Locomotive Engineers & Firemen (ASLEF), so some very interesting discussions took place during the evenings. Although neither of us visualised it at the time, our differing loyalties were to come into conflict at a later date.

My training commenced with a period in the depot office learning the basic workings from the chief clerk. I was introduced to the 'Conditions of Service' books for footplate and conciliation staff; I had never realised that things could be so complicated when firemen were seeking promotion to driving positions. Driver vacancies were advertised bi-monthly with positions being filled on the basis of 'preference or accommodation moves and seniority'. Firemen applying for driving positions had to list depots in order of preference, but could make their first choice one where there was no current vacancy. I well recall one particular instance where a fireman listed his preferences in the wrong order and denied himself getting a driving position at the depot where he wished to finish his career.

While I was aware of the general geography of the South Eastern and Central Divisions of the Southern Region, I was also coming across new locations such as Rotherhithe Road, Mercers Crossing, Angerstein Wharf and Ewer Street. During this period in the general office I was also introduced to the running foremen, the roster clerks, and to Charlie Richford, who was in charge of the staff in the Maintenance Shop where 'classified' repairs were undertaken.

In view of my interest in rides on the footplate I was highly delighted when, a few days after arriving at Bricklayers Arms, I was issued with a footplate pass that covered the whole of the South Eastern Division. I made as much use of this facility as possible in order to obtain an insight into the workings of locomotives and multiple units and to build up a fairly comprehensive knowledge of the various routes of the Division.

My next move was to the roster clerk's office to become familiar with the rostering arrangements, the routes covered by the footplate staff at 'The Brick', and the rules governing the use of 'passed firemen' (those eligible also to drive). At many depots the latter could only be rostered for a driving job appropriate to the shift they were on. However, at 'The Brick' local agreements allowed passed firemen to move from early to late shift or vice versa provided that they had the requisite 12 hours rest between shifts.

Most of the drivers and passed firemen had route knowledge over the whole of the South Eastern and Central Divisions, so coverage of special workings did not cause too much of a problem. Although the fleet of steam locomotives was decreasing rapidly, training for footplate staff on diesel and electric locomotives and on diesel multiple units was well advanced. Some of the passed firemen had also been trained to cover electric multiple units and 'The Brick' was used as a cover depot for EMU working when shortages arose at the central roster office at London Bridge.

As Bricklayers Arms depot was due to close at the end of 1961 there was a severe shortage of drivers, so many of the passed firemen were regularly working as drivers. Although I was only there a few months I found most of the footplate staff at the depot very reliable and co-operative.

While the problems of drinking on duty have only hit the headlines in more recent times, it was fairly common knowledge that some footplate staff did enjoy a 'pint' during their turn of duty and I have heard many comments made that certain drivers were much better at their job in these circumstances. However, there was one incident that I recall when a certain passed fireman, while working as a driver, was arrested following an incident in the Gillingham area. Although he was subjected to the Disciplinary Procedure and dismissed from the service, he was subsequently reinstated only to be involved in a serious derailment some years later when it was suggested that he had been drinking in a club at Ramsgate during his break.

Even the shedmaster and mechanical foreman at 'The Brick' were known for their lunchtime visits to The Swan hostelry for a pint or two. On their return the shedmaster would retire to his office and would not be seen again until about 4 o'clock, when he would shave and sign the outgoing correspondence.

During my spell at 'The Brick' my oldest daughter was born. When Charles Boarer heard that my wife had gone into hospital for the imminent birth he insisted that I should catch the first train home and travel back to Salisbury each evening for the period my wife was in hospital. To celebrate my daughter's birth I invited certain members of the staff for a celebratory drink, and it was very strange that the one person who forgot the occasion was the shedmaster!

One incident that arose while I was at Bricklayers Arms relates to a driver who decided to buy a greyhound. Being on shift work meant that it was not always possible for him to attend the local race meetings. However, it so happened that he was due for a routine medical examination, the depot being subsequently advised that he had fallen below the standard required for his current work. This meant allocation to a 'restricted' driving position in the depot where he did not have to work shifts. As the closure of Bricklayers Arms approached, arrangements were being made to transfer staff to other depots of their choice. Unfortunately the number of restricted driving positions was limited, so the driver in question requested a further medical examination and, lo and behold, was then found to be fit for main-line work! Whether the greyhound was a winner or not I do not know.

After my spell with the roster clerk I went with the motive power foremen, who were responsible for the daily operation of the depot, ensuring that locomotives were allocated to services and making alterations to cover staff not available for their rostered work due to sickness or extended hours on a previous working. In the latter days of steam operation locomotive failures were becoming a regular feature, so the work of the motive power foremen became more difficult.

While I was satisfied with my lodgings I wanted a place where my wife and daughter could join me. As the railways still owned a lot of property I applied for various vacant accommodation and eventually obtained a ground floor flat at Kent House station where my family joined me at the end of October. The flat was part of the old station master's house, the upper floor being occupied by Don Pullen, an EMU driver at Victoria. Eventually Don became Assistant General Secretary of ASLEF when Ray Buckton was General Secretary, and in subsequent years, after we left the flat, Don and I met on numerous social and work occasions.

During my time at Bricklayers Arms I managed to attend four major derailments, one at Coulsdon North, two at Farningham Road and one at the 'Dust' sidings near the latter station.

In the incident at Coulsdon North an EMU had been derailed on a set of catch points and was leaning towards the edge of the embankment so it had to be shored up with timber before re-railing operations, could commence.

The second derailment involved a train of 'vanfits' on the down line at Farningham Road. One of the wagons had suffered a fractured wheelset, causing a number of wagons to be derailed and serious damage to about a mile of track. On arrival at the site we examined the derailed wagons and found the fractured wheelset by the side of the track but could not find the wagon to which it belonged. Eventually, after quite a long search, we spotted it lying in the garden of a bungalow some 50 feet below the railway. Descending the embankment to assess the damage, we spoke to the owner who said that she was hanging out the washing when she heard a loud noise and, on looking up, saw the wagon literally flying through the air. She then went indoors and telephoned her husband to say, 'It has happened.' It appears that the couple had been expecting just such an incident ever since they arrived at the bungalow.

The second derailment at Farningham Road was on the up line and involved a train of Transfesa wagons loaded with fruit and

The incident at Coulsdon North in which an electric multiple unit was derailed at a set of catch points. *Author*

vegetables. In this incident a number of wagons were derailed causing the coupling between the first and second wagon to break.

Normally in such circumstances the fracturing of the brake pipe would apply the brakes on the locomotive and train, but due to a defective 'air-vacuum' relay valve on the locomotive this did not happen and the train only came to a stand when the driver noticed that he had lost traction current. When we arrived at the scene we found the area literally covered in crushed fruit and vegetables.

Refuse from the Camberwell area of London was loaded into mineral wagons at the Elephant & Castle sidings, which were then conveyed to a refuse tip near Farningham Road. On arrival at the site the locomotive propelled the wagons into refuge sidings from whence they were moved by tractor to the point of discharge. On one occasion a raft of wagons ran away and became derailed at the end of a siding where there were no buffer stops. As can be imagined, the ground in a refuse tip is not firm enough to allow the use of a crane or jacks and packing, so it was decided to try to haul the derailed wagons back towards the main line where the ground was much firmer. Some of the nearer wagons were recovered successfully, but during attempts to recover the last two a chain broke and the broken link just missed a member of the breakdown crew. In the end it was deemed safer to leave these two wagons to be broken up for scrap.

With the imminent closure of Bricklayers Arms and the elimination of steam on the South Eastern Division I was concerned about my own position. However, this concern proved unfounded as I was advised that I would transfer to Hither Green to continue my training in January 1962. When I arrived there I found a modernised depot that had undergone many changes to enable it to cope with the ever-increasing fleet of diesel-electric locomotives.

Under the British Railways Modernisation Plan the Southern Region had opted for a fleet of Type 3 1550hp diesel-electric. These were numbered in the D65XX series, eventually being renumbered 33XXX to meet the requirements of the computerised TOPS system where every locomotive had to be allocated a five-digit number.

New locomotives were being delivered to Hither Green at the rate of one each week, and when I arrived some of the earlier ones were going back to Birmingham for modifications. The normal practice was that the crew would depart on Thursdays with the locomotive for modification and return the following day with a new one. As Hither Green drivers only 'knew the road' as far as Kensington Olympia, they were scheduled to pick up a pilotman at Kensington.

An interesting story concerned a Hither Green driver who picked up the pilotman at Kensington on one journey in very thick fog. As the pilotman was unfamiliar with the locomotive it was his responsibility to advise the Hither Green driver of speed restrictions and signal placings along the route. After the signal cleared for departure from Kensington, the pilotman was talking and looking round the cab. After a while he asked the Hither Green driver where the automatic train control (ATC) equipment was and was advised that these engines were only fitted with the BR AWS system. This resulted in a sudden concentration on the track for the rest of the journey!

The GWR had introduced a system of automatic train control many years ago based on giving drivers audible advice on the position of Distant signals. Physical contact between the locomotive and a ramp between the running lines gave a bell signal in the cab if the Distant was in the clear position. A horn sounded if the signal was 'on', and the brakes were applied if it was not cancelled. In the 1950s BR began experiments with an alternative system that provided the same audio indication without any physical contact, thus eliminating wear on the ramp and the pick-up shoe. The BR system also used a dial in the cab to give an ongoing reminder of the position of the last Distant signal. I often wonder whether the incident at Kensington was an instance where a driver had previously relied fully on the ATC system when it should have been used only as an aid to driving.

In addition to our fleet of Type 3 locomotives, three Type 2s of the D5000 class had been borrowed from the Eastern Region for specific services that required steam heating. Hither Green staff were responsible for scheduling and undertaking examinations for the whole fleet and, since all the Type 3s worked only within the South Eastern Division, only fuelling, water, oil checks and minor repairs were carried out at such places as Faversham, Ashford and Tonbridge.

In this period of changeover from steam to electric and diesel traction most of the passenger train workings from Charing Cross, Cannon Street, London Bridge, Blackfriars/Holborn Viaduct and Victoria were covered by EMUs or diesel-electric multiple units (DEMUs). However, there were still a few locomotive-hauled services, the 'Golden Arrow' and 'Night Ferry' being hauled by electric locomotives of the E5000 class. Problems arose with the 4.56pm service from Cannon Street to Ramsgate, for while a Type 3 was adequate for traction purposes, a Type 2 with a steam heating boiler had to be used due to insufficient numbers of electrically-heated coaches.

Although the 'Night Ferry' was scheduled to be hauled by an electric locomotive these tended to suffer loss of power and adhesion problems when the weather was very frosty or damp or when there were leaves on the rails in autumn. Then two Type 3 machines were substituted. All freight and parcels trains had electric or diesel-electric locomotives, the former being controlled and maintained by Stewarts Lane depot, which also inherited the Bricklayers Arms steam crane.

After my first week at Hither Green I went on a four-week intensive diesel course at the School of Transport at Derby. I found this very beneficial as there was a good balance between theoretical and practical work. We also spent a considerable amount of time on fault-finding on locomotives and multiple units, the faults having been 'created' by the instructors. I recall two of these faults, one on a multiple unit and the other on an English Electric shunting locomotive. In the first case the float switch contacts in the water header tank, designed to prevent an engine from being started if there was a shortage of water, had been reversed so that when the water was low the engine would start normally. As we had been taught to check water and oil levels before starting an engine, adding water just

created the wrong indication. In the case of the shunting locomotive, tape had been placed over the starting contactors so that when they closed no current passed and the engine would not start.

On my return to Hither Green I spent three months with Mechanical Foreman Jack Brewer and his maintenance staff carrying out repairs and examinations. This was followed by a spell with the motive power foremen working the three shifts. It was during this period that I witnessed the makings of what could have been a serious accident at St Johns where the line from Lewisham joins those from Hither Green.

Early one evening a telephone call reported the failure of a diesel-electric locomotive at the country end of the down main platform at St Johns. I persuaded the motive power foreman to let me accompany the maintenance staff that were sent by locomotive to assist. On arrival we stopped at the country end of the up main platform so that both main lines were now blocked and all trains were diverted to the relief lines. An examination of the failed locomotive quickly revealed that its fuel tank was empty. Arrangements were then made for our locomotive to proceed to North Kent East Junction, cross there to the down main and return to St Johns to couple to the failed machine. As the two locomotives were electrically compatible it would be possible for them to be driven from the failed unit.

While we were waiting for the assisting locomotive to return from crossing over I was standing on the platform talking to the driver of the failed engine and could see an EMU train, which had already passed the junction signal, approaching from the Lewisham direction. To my great concern I then saw a parcels train approaching at speed on the up slow. Collision seemed a real possibility, but fortunately the driver of the Lewisham train spotted the parcels service and managed to bring his train to a stand just short of the junction. I subsequently learned that the driver of the parcels train had passed a signal at danger. After an inquiry he was disciplined and taken off main-line driving for a long period. We got our failed locomotive back to Hither Green without further incident.

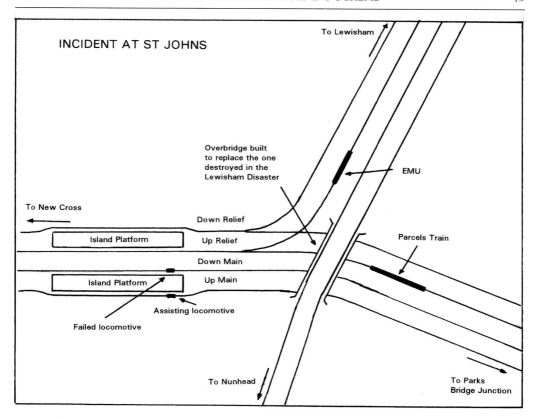

INCIDENT AT ST JOHNS

To Lewisham

Overbridge built
to replace the one
destroyed in the
Lewisham Disaster

EMU

To New Cross

Down Relief

Island Platform   Up Relief   Parcels Train

Down Main

Island Platform   Up Main

Assisting locomotive

Failed locomotive

To Nunhead   To Parks
                                                     Bridge Junction

While a programme had been drawn up for my training it had been explained at one of my 'progress' interviews that it might be varied from time to time. I was not surprised, therefore, to be called to London Bridge to discuss a special assignment. At the time running trials were being undertaken with the first two electro-diesel locomotives, which were basically an electric locomotive provided with a small diesel engine that could be used for power on lines with no conductor rail. These were ideal for the Southern Region with its third rail electrification and enjoyed the additional benefit of being able to work during engineering operations when lines were still open to traffic but the electrical supply had been switched off.

The reason for my call to London Bridge soon became clear. The Drivers' Training School, based at Stewarts Lane, was in the process of preparing training material for the first courses on electro-diesel locomotives.

The technical data was being supplied by the Chief Mechanical & Electrical Engineer's department, but someone was needed to prepare drawings showing the layout and position of the various components in the control gear and the brake, fuel and cooling systems. As I had passed examinations in technical drawing I was quite interested in undertaking the work. I was allocated an office at Stewarts Lane, in one of the arches that carried the South London lines over the depot, and for about six weeks I worked on the drawings. Some may have found this boring but I enjoyed it, especially as there was the opportunity to go out on some trial runs. Railwaymen have always used what may be considered rather strange terminology, and it was on one of these trial runs that I first heard of a signal showing two yellow lights being referred to as 'two chinamen'.

When the work at Stewarts Lane was finished I moved on to the next spell of training, in the motive power office at London Bridge. As there were only six shedmasters in the SE Division this office had a fairly small complement of staff who looked after such things as 'Lost Time Tickets', derailment and incident reports, failure of locomotives or units under the Casualty Reporting system, availability and utilisation returns, ordering and supply of fuel and oil, and disciplinary matters.

Having always considered punctuality to be important, I was interested in what happened to Lost Time Tickets sent out to the depots for completion by drivers. On return these were collated by cause – traction unit failure, traction unit late from depot or holding siding, signal failure, relieving staff not available on time, etc. Regular discussions were then held with the technical departments to try to eliminate repetitive delays. One thing I did think was a waste of time was pursuing cases of a train late in passing one of its reporting points but still arriving on or before its scheduled time.

The work in the motive power office seemed quite varied to someone like myself, only there in a temporary capacity, but I suspect it would get monotonous to anyone there on a permanent basis. Being a trainee I had the advantage of being able to go into other offices to meet traffic staff involved in day-to-day operating matters. In this process I met Chief District Inspector Bert Harding, a marvellous character with a wealth of experience, and through him learned a lot about the signalling side of the business. He was always willing to discuss things with me and on a number of occasions I went out with him when signal sighting issues were to be discussed.

The six shedmasters in the South Eastern Division – Charles Boarer, who had moved to London Bridge, Cedric Knott of Hither Green, Ted Wardman of Tonbridge, Derek Mitchell of Ashford, Bob Bates of Faversham, and Bob Easton of Dover – all attended regular meetings with the Motive Power Officer and his assistants. I was able to attend many of these meetings and learn at first hand the nature of the real, everyday problems with which the shedmasters had to deal. An example was the serious staff shortages being faced by many depots, and one of the most important things to come out of these meetings concerned ways of overcoming the consequent difficulties. It appeared that most staff fell into one of three categories, those to whom one could suggest ways of covering vacancies, those who could be asked to assist, and those who had to be directed.

After the period at London Bridge I moved on to the Line Traffic Manager's office at Queen Street. This dealt with staff matters such as promotional arrangements, accommodation, matters that could not be resolved by the Local Departmental Committees and therefore had to be discussed at Sectional Council, appeals against punishment given under the disciplinary procedure, the issue of uniform clothing, and travel facilities. Then it was back to the real world of railways with a spell at the Diesel-Electric Multiple Unit Maintenance Depot at St Leonards, Hastings. The depot master there taught me something I have never forgotten: 'Never use long words in letters as the recipient may not understand their meaning and in some cases you might not either!'

The DEMUs were used for the services between London and Hastings and were similar in design to those on the Salisbury-Portsmouth services. The main difference was that the Hastings units were built to a restricted width to allow them to pass through Mountfield Tunnel. They also operated in six-car formations whereas the units used between Salisbury and Portsmouth were worked in threes.

At the start of my training I was told that it would be for a period of up to two years and was surprised to receive a telephone call from Jack Morris at London Bridge asking why I had not applied for the vacancy as shedmaster at Dover. I explained that I thought it would be premature to apply for promotion after little more than 12 months, but the response was that I was considered suitable and should therefore submit my application. I did so, was interviewed and, to my delight, was informed that I had been appointed. My training would cease at the end of November and I would then take up my new position. In the meantime I set about learning as much as I could of the responsibilities of the new post.

4
SHEDMASTER AT DOVER

In the few weeks that remained of my training I was able to obtain some general information about the scope and responsibilities of my new position at Dover. The office was situated in Dover Town Yard near the beach and I was told that it could get very cold in winter. My main responsibility was the provision of train crews for a variety of services from the Dover and Ramsgate areas, and to meet this requirement there was a staff of over 300 spread between five locations: Dover Marine (later Western Docks), Dover Priory, Ramsgate, Margate and Folkestone Junction (later East). Although train crew rosters and timesheets were dealt with at Ashford for Dover, and Faversham for Ramsgate/Margate, the day-to-day running of the area was in the hands of motive power foremen based at Dover and Ramsgate, with leading drivers at Dover Priory and Margate. A Locomotive Inspector, directly responsible to the Motive Power Officer, was based at Ramsgate, while a clerk with an office at Dover Priory dealt with general correspondence, stores ordering, travel facilities and welfare matters.

Drivers based at Margate and Dover Priory worked EMU trains over all routes between Dover, Ramsgate and Margate and Victoria, Charing Cross, Cannon Street and Blackfriars/Holborn Viaduct.

Folkestone Junction depot was staffed by three drivers who worked the local yard pilot, while Dover Marine and Ramsgate were classified as mixed traction depots. The difference between the two was that Dover Marine staff were mainly involved in freight train working, although they did cover the 'Night Ferry' and 'Golden Arrow' services and a few parcels trains, whereas the staff at Ramsgate were mainly on EMU workings. Both depots had a small complement of passed firemen and there were a number of passed cleaners at Dover Marine depot.

To provide complete flexibility in the South Eastern Division its drivers had to be conversant with all routes. This meant that they had to work over a route at least once in six months to maintain their route knowledge, and while this caused some complications the benefits were seen when trains had to be diverted, as no pilotman was needed.

Senior Motive Power Foreman Bob Easton had been covering the vacancy at Dover between the retirement of the previous shedmaster and my own arrival. He spent the first week with me before resuming his normal duties and also welcomed me to stay with him and his wife until I could find more permanent accommodation. I gladly accepted the offer and once again found lodgings were I was treated as one of the family.

During the first week I met some of my supervisors, staff representatives and train crews, including Driver George Primmer, who had previously been a passed fireman at Salisbury. I also got to know the area by identifying such locations as Bulwark Street, Ferry Sidings, Admiralty Sidings, Calais End, Gas Works Siding and Folkestone Harbour Station. In practice, with a staff of over 300 and no maintenance responsibilities, the Dover shedmaster's job was largely taken up with staff and administration matters, including discipline, safety and timekeeping.

At any BR locations with more than 50

people in a single group of grades, the staff were entitled to elect four members to represent them in discussions with management on a Local Departmental Committee (LDC); locations with less than 50 staff could elect two 'staff representatives'. The items discussed fell into two categories. 'Consultation' items were generally those where management was advancing ideas for future developments, while 'Negotiation' covered day-to-day matters like link working and rosters. If agreement could not be reached in the latter area, either side could refer the matter to the Sectional Council, the next level in the Machinery of Negotiation. The minutes of these bodies formed a sort of case book law and were signed, numbered and published on depot notice boards.

I have always found that one of the easiest ways of finding out where major problems had arisen in the past was to read the LDC minutes for the location. To my astonishment, when I read the minutes for Dover Marine I found that there were over 800, with the first one being over 40 years old! Clearly many of them were no longer relevant since they referred to the steam era or to drivers who had now retired, so at my first meeting with the LDC I suggested a progressive review and removal of the outdated items. One particular minute, drawn up in the early days of the Second World War, gave details of the action to be taken in the event of an invasion. Locomotives were to be immobilised by placing sand in the bearings or spanners or other objects down the blastpipe!

Discipline in the Dover area was very good. Unlike London, where some staff had to leave their homes 2 hours before starting duty, most of the Dover staff lived locally and punctuality was not a problem. Most of the disciplinary cases involved operational matters such as signals passed at danger, failing to stop at a station or causing a derailment or collision.

The railway disciplinary procedure began with a verbal warning, followed by a written warning. Subsequent misdemeanours were dealt with by the issue of a Form 1, specifying the charge and to which the response could either be in writing or by interview. At an interview the defendant could be represented either by a fellow employee or, as was usually the case, by an officer of his trade union. The punishments, notified using a Form 2, could be a reprimand, a severe reprimand, reduction in grade, removal from current duties, or suspension, with suspensions for more then seven days accompanied by a final warning. Appeals against a punishment awarded locally went to the Motive Power Officer.

As shedmaster I could not issue a Form 1, but did award punishment at the first level. In one case at Dover a driver who had requested a personal interview for a Form 1 hearing arrived with my uncle as his representative. We agreed that it would be wrong for two members of a family to be dealing with the case, and arranged for another shedmaster to undertake the hearing.

Being responsible for a large organisation, I began by seeing all the correspondence before deciding what could be delegated and what I needed to see on a regular basis. I could see the reasons for the monthly 'Availability and Utilisation Return', as this helped to determine the numbers required to cover allocated duties, but some other items appeared less than essential. Among these was the reporting to the motive power office of the daily arrival times of the 'Golden Arrow'. This had been instituted in a period of bad timekeeping and never rescinded, despite the fact that no one looked at the figures any longer. They were stopped.

While checking timesheets at the end of my second week at Dover I noticed that my clerk had been claiming overtime. Since we had to cut expenditure I told him that he would need my authority for this in future. He did not appreciate my view on this issue and later resigned. As no relief clerk was available I undertook the clerk's duties in addition to my own and, despite a 'dead slow' typing speed, managed to keep ahead of the work.

Ever since my arrival I had been curious about the locked cupboard in the clerk's office. Along with his work I had also inherited his keys, and now had the opportunity to satisfy my curiosity. On opening the cupboard I was amazed to find it filled with stationery in quantities that were to supply the Dover requirement for the whole of

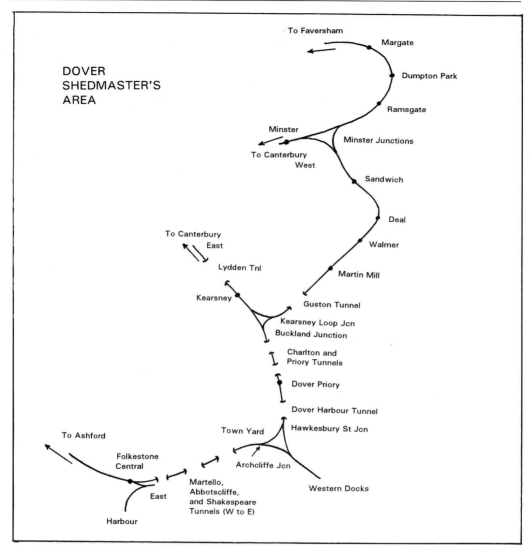

DOVER
SHEDMASTER'S
AREA

To Faversham

Margate

Dumpton Park

Ramsgate

Minster

Minster Junctions

To Canterbury
West

Sandwich

Deal

To Canterbury
East

Walmer

Lydden Tnl

Martin Mill

Kearsney

Guston Tunnel

Kearsney Loop Jcn

Buckland Junction

Charlton and
Priory Tunnels

Dover Priory

Dover Harbour Tunnel

Town Yard

Hawkesbury St Jcn

To Ashford

Folkestone
Central

Archcliffe Jcn

Martello,
Abbotscliffe,
and Shakespeare
Tunnels (W to E)

East

Western Docks

Harbour

my time there. I also found long outdated items such as metal tubes for using up pencil stubs, boxes of pen nibs, pen-holders and piles of obsolete forms. Even more astonishing were the price lists on the back of each cupboard door. These covered a variety of food items such as tins of meat and vegetables, enquiries revealing that my clerk had a nice little sideline in buying goods in bulk and selling them as single items!

On 31 December 1962 the location of the shedmaster's office was moved to platform 5/6 at Dover Marine station. What a day it turned out to be! Overnight snow had fallen heavily and moving office equipment in heavy snow is not something I would recommend. At least when the move was over we had much more comfortable accommodation. Little did anyone realise that this was the start of a very severe cold spell that would bring three months of operating problems.

In the first week of January 1963 serious delays were affecting all services due to frozen points, ice on conductor rails and snowdrifts.

An independent snow plough, propelled by an 'H' Class 0-4-4 tank engine, was in regular use between Ashford and Hastings, with diesel-electric locomotives fitted with miniature snow ploughs running over other routes. The problem of snow was compounded by high winds blowing the snow into the area's numerous cuttings. In the very low temperatures diesel fuel was turning to jelly and had to be drained from the fuel tanks as, even when heated, it would not revert to its original liquid form. Due to ice on the conductor rail the first EMU trains over each route out of Dover had to be assisted by diesel-electric locomotives.

Further problems arose one morning when an electrical short circuit closed the whole of the Dover Priory station area. During routine track examination a member of the permanent way staff had dropped a spanner on to the conductor rail and one running rail. A great flash, which fortunately caused no injuries, illuminated the whole of the station, and the traction current could not be restored until safety checks had been carried out. Unfortunately the Dover Priory area still had semaphore signalling, and where signal wires ran beneath the lines they had been destroyed by the short circuit.

I well remember an incident during this spell of extreme weather when I was returning from home to Dover one morning. I caught a local service from Kent House to Bromley where there was a connection with a main-line train to Dover. The journey was uneventful until we reached Faversham, but on leaving there the train really struggled on the incline to Selling and eventually stopped just in advance of a set of catch points. We knew that if we slipped backwards derailment was a possibility, so assistance was requested. Eventually a diesel-electric locomotive arrived.

The plan was that this would propel us to Canterbury East, run round the train, then haul us to Dover. However, we almost missed stopping at Canterbury East because the driver on the assisting locomotive had forgotten to isolate his brake valve, which meant that when the EMU driver applied the brake to reduce the brake pipe pressure, the assisting locomotive was promptly recharging it. We only stopped when the EMU driver used the emergency brake position.

My one regret at Dover was that there was no breakdown train, as I loved the challenge of the re-railing operations and of determining the cause of a derailment. When the motive power depot had closed after the withdrawal of steam, the breakdown train had been scrapped and arrangements made to cover the area from either Ashford or Faversham. Fortunately we did not have too many derailments, but there were a couple of incidents, which we managed to overcome without assistance.

The first derailment happened about 4 o'clock on Christmas Eve 1962 when an empty Transfesa wagon became derailed between the Ferry sidings and Hawkesbury Street signal box. The incident completely blocked all movements on to or off the train ferry ships and could not be left until after the Christmas break. With the help of the local Carriage & Wagon staff and a set of re-railing ramps we managed to re-rail the wagon, examine it, gauge the wheels, then place the vehicle on the Dunkirk ship. All was then clear for the outbound evening sleeping cars for Paris and Brussels.

Although I never heard any direct comments about this incident, I was at a routine shedmasters' meeting some months later when the Motive Power Officer asked if there had been any Dover derailments when the Ashford breakdown train had not been requested. It appeared that someone at Ashford had found out about the incident and claimed the breakdown allowance of 4s 6d. I confessed my part in the event, but there was no criticism and I doubt whether the Ashford staff got their money!

The second derailment involved a Motor Luggage Van that had arrived at Dover attached to an EMU set; many trains conveyed MLVs to make up for the limited luggage space on the electric multiple units. They were like passenger coaches but without seats, and had traction motors plus rechargeable batteries to allow them to go into non-electrified areas.

I received information from the station

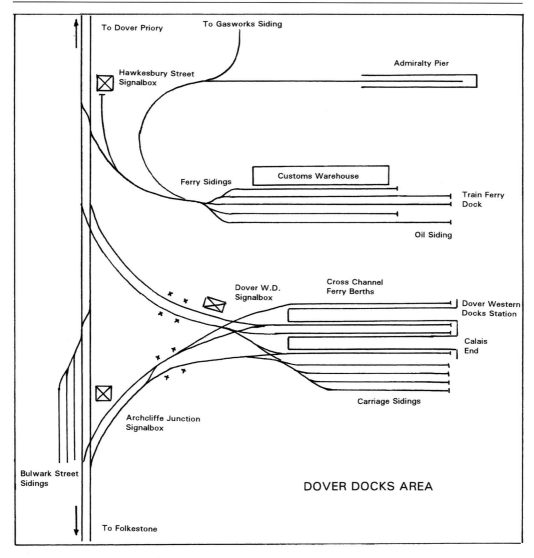

To Dover Priory

To Gasworks Siding

Admiralty Pier

Hawkesbury Street
Signalbox

Ferry Sidings

Customs Warehouse

Train Ferry
Dock

Oil Siding

Dover W.D.
Signalbox

Cross Channel
Ferry Berths

Dover Western
Docks Station

Calais
End

Carriage Sidings

Archcliffe Junction
Signalbox

Bulwark Street
Sidings

DOVER DOCKS AREA

To Folkestone

master that an MLV had been derailed on the quayside. He asked if I would assess the situation as it would take at least an hour before the Ashford breakdown train could get to Dover. I agreed to meet him at the site of the derailment, where I found that only one pair of wheels was derailed and the vehicle was adjacent to one of the dockside cranes. Knowing the capacity of this and that the MLV was empty, arrangements were made to obtain the services of a qualified crane driver. The crane hook was lowered and placed in the

vehicle coupling. The lift took place, the wheels were gauged and we all pushed the vehicle until it was positioned above the track for lowering. After examination by the C&W staff the vehicle was declared safe to run and duly made its rostered return trip to Victoria.

All shedmasters in the South Eastern Division were technically trained and given practical driving experience on the various forms of traction operated by their staff. Whenever I made journeys from Dover I always tried to travel with the drivers. Not only did this help me get to know the area and my staff, but also let the latter know that I was interested in their work.

When attending meetings in London I always travelled in the cab of the locomotive hauling the inbound 'Night Ferry' service. The train was scheduled to leave Dover Marine at 7.20am, but if the ship from Dunkirk was delayed the departure was put back to 8.05. Due to the intensive suburban service operated on the South Eastern Division and the importance of the 'Night Ferry', the 7.20 routing was via Chatham and the later path via Ashford. The experience of travelling on, and on occasions driving, an electric locomotive at 90mph with a train weighing up to 850 tons is one I shall always remember. Little did I think that I should later enjoy the benefits of travelling between European capitals on this train.

In February 1963, when my wife was expecting our second child, I bought a house on the outskirts of Dover, so once again my family were able to join me and we soon settled into 84 Markland Road.

Prior to this move I had only been able to get home at weekends and my wife had been living in a flat without running water. The pipes had frozen during the prolonged cold spell so I had to fill the bath from a standpipe at weekends to enable my wife to get through the following week.

During my spell at Dover I learned a lot about the different types of people in the organisation. Most were very responsible and willing to go to great lengths to maintain the service that the public was seeking. Just a few had to be watched fairly closely to make sure they did their job properly.

If everything ran smoothly all the time it would be a very boring existence, and this was never the case at any of the depots where I was in charge. Dover was no exception, and while travelling with one EMU driver I had to remind him that the Forward/Reverse lever must never be put in mid-position as this had the effect of isolating the 'dead man's handle' safety device. In the complement of drivers at Dover Marine depot there were two brothers. The older brother was the type who came to work, did his duty, then went home, and I can

never recall having to talk to him about any incident. Unfortunately the younger brother was one of those people whom misfortune seemed to follow. As an example, on one particular evening he was working an electric locomotive from Dover to Hither Green to pick up a train of empty Transfesa wagons that were urgently wanted on the Continent. While passing through Shepherdswell Tunnel the locomotive failed about a hundred yards from Shepherdswell station, which had a signal box from which assistance could have been summoned quickly. For some reason, which he was quite unable to explain, the driver walked the other way, towards Dover, and had to trudge 3 miles before he came to a signal box.

Another incident also involved Transfesa wagons, but on this occasion they were loaded. The train was the 8.58am from Dover to Hither Green Continental Sidings routed via Chatham. For the first few miles there were no problems, but on approaching Adisham the driver, Ray Keeler, saw that the Distant signal was in the caution position and began to apply the brake. As the train approached the Home signal, which was at danger, the driver realised that he was not going to stop and quickly placed the valve in the emergency position. Even this failed to do the trick, and the train passed the Home, the Starter and travelled some way towards the next station before it eventually came to a stand.

The train was formed of 24 dual-braked wagons and a vacuum-braked bogie brake-van, and was being operated under the vacuum brake system. An on-the-spot examination was carried out to determine why it had failed to stop, but a brake continuity test showed that all pipes were correctly coupled and the vacuum gauge in the brake-van was showing the correct level.

Next a number of handbrakes were applied, a driver's brake valve application made and a check carried out on each wagon to ascertain whether the brake was working. It was – but only on the locomotive, four wagons and the brake-van. To prevent further delays it was agreed to move the train, at very slow speed, to Faversham for more extensive examination. This revealed that somewhere on the journey from Spain the vacuum brakes had been isolated on 20 wagons but no Brake Defect labels had been placed on the wagons or other advice given.

In addition to the brake problem the inspections revealed that certain wagon springs seemed to be under extreme pressure and arrangements were made to have some vehicles weighed. These wagons had a carrying capacity of 26 tons and a tare weight of 14 tons, but the weighing showed that many of them were overloaded by as much as 10 tons. Clearly the procedures needed tightening up and instructions were issued to ensure a complete check on all Continental arrivals with especial attention to the vacuum brake, particularly as many of the Continental systems used the air brake system.

I have mentioned previously the importance attached to the running of the 'Golden Arrow' service. One morning the train was running about 20 minutes late and Control asked me to see the driver and ascertain the reason. When the train arrived I spoke to the driver and asked for a report giving the reasons for the delay. Later he came to my office with his report, which stated that the 'overload' on the electric locomotive had operated three times during the journey. On the first two occasion he had been able to reset it from the button in the cab, but the third time he had to go to the control cabinet inside the locomotive.

I knew that if the report went to the motive power office at London Bridge someone would be aware that the train had been operated by a driver only and would want to know where it had stopped to allow him to leave the cab. When I asked this question I was astounded to be told that the driver had not stopped when he left his cab and the train had thus been travelling at speeds up to 90 mph with no one at the controls and the dead man's handle out of use. The consequences could have been disastrous, and while I appreciated that Harry was motivated by avoiding delay, I thought it prudent for him to write out a fresh report saying that the overload had operated three times and then held after the third reset. This is what went to London Bridge and nothing further was heard of the matter.

While locomotive failures were rare during my period at Dover, I did experience a problem when travelling back from Salisbury one Sunday evening. My wife and daughters were staying in Salisbury for a few days so I was alone and, after a chat with the driver, Bert Hooker of Nine Elms, I settled down to read a book. I was surprised when the train stopped at Whitchurch North station as this was not a booked stop; I then learned from the guard that the locomotive had failed.

The guard and I alighted and walked along the platform to the locomotive, where I found the driver in the engine compartment. He revealed that the transmission defect light on one engine had indicated a fault and he was trying to isolate the transmission unit. The guard went off to advise the signalman of the situation, while between us Bert and I managed to isolate the defective unit. Fortunately these engines had two power units and by the time the guard returned we were ready to proceed on one. We arrived in Waterloo some 30 minutes late, but I am sure we would have been much later if we had had to wait for another locomotive.

After I had been at Dover for some nine months I considered myself fully capable of all the duties there and began to take an interest in the weekly vacancy list. In the space of four weeks shedmaster's jobs at Severn Tunnel Junction, Tyne Dock, Southall and Guildford were advertised, and I applied for them all.

The interview for the Tyne Dock vacancy in the motive power office at Newcastle Central station was one of the most pleasant I ever had. I arrived early, was seen promptly at 2 o'clock and immediately offered tea and biscuits. The questions on my experience and ideas for the future lasted a gruelling hour and a half, but I felt that the whole proceedings were very thorough.

Back at Dover I started to scan the incoming mail with increasing interest and was delighted when a letter arrived advising me that I had been appointed to the position at Tyne Dock and should report on 2 December.

I planned a week's leave before going to Tyne Dock, but early in November I received notification of interviews for the Southall and

Guildford positions during the week I was on leave. As these were one grade higher than the post at Tyne Dock I saw no reason why I should not attend.

When I arrived at Paddington for the interview for the job at Southall I found that I was the last person to be interviewed; the interview was 40 minutes later than planned and then only lasted 10 minutes. When I compared this with the length of interview at Newcastle I did not rate my chances too highly. However, the following morning a messenger arrived at my house with a note asking me to telephone the motive power office. I did this from the station and was very surprised to be congratulated on my appointment as the next shedmaster at Southall. Some months later I learned from the retiring Motive Power Officer that I would not have gone to Tyne Dock anyway because if I had not been appointed to Southall I would have got the Guildford job. It appeared that my future had already been planned for me!

5
THE WESTERN REGION

As the arrangements for my promotion to the position of shedmaster at Southall had progressed so quickly, I did not have time to find out much about the depot before taking over. In December 1963 I reported to Divisional Maintenance Engineer Bill Sidwell at Paddington, met various members of his staff and was then accompanied to Southall by Divisional Locomotive Engineer Peter Sutton. Although I did not know it at the time, many of the people I met at Paddington on my first day on the Western Region were to remain close working colleagues throughout my subsequent career.

The journey to Southall was short, and soon, as the train approached Southall station, I had my first glimpse of the location I was to manage for the next two years. From the station we made our way past Southall Station signal box and via the official walking route to the depot.

The first functional point we came to was the water softening plant; later I was to learn that climbing to the top gave one a marvellous panoramic view over West London. Then came my first view of the depot proper, from the western end. Ahead was the diesel multiple unit (DMU) maintenance shed with two roads and adjacent to a siding that ran parallel to the down main line. On the right was the area where steam locomotives were maintained, while the offices and messrooms were on the south side of the depot. Although the diesel shed had doors, the steam shed was open at both ends and was a very cold place to work during the winter.

My office was at the east end of the depot next to the one used by the motive power foremen. The turntable was at the extreme eastern end where the boundary wall separated us from a factory that made parts for the diesel engines used on DMUs and buses.

Adjacent was the drop-pit shed and the boiler house, which provided depot heating and the hot water used for boiler washing. The branch line to Brentford Dock ran along the southern edge of the depot behind the coal stage and a few sidings used for storage purposes. To minimise the cost of water from the mains, a pumping station alongside the Brentford branch drew water from a well and provided the main supply for the water softening plant.

Maintenance facilities were provided at three points within the depot. Examinations and repairs on steam locomotives were carried out in the main part, while those on DMUs and diesel-electric shunters were undertaken in the diesel shed. Repairs requiring the removal of a wheelset or involving work on valves or pistons were carried out in the drop-pit shop, which also had facilities for machining steam chests and cylinder liners. While all the fitters in the diesel shed had served an apprenticeship, many of those on the steam locomotives were 'dilutees', ie men who had not served an apprenticeship but were considered competent by virtue of their experience.

I was shown my office by senior Motive Power Foreman Ivor Imm, who had run the depot while the shedmaster's position was vacant and who was to remain with me for my first week. He came from the Welsh valleys and had progressed through the footplate grades and into supervisory positions on his

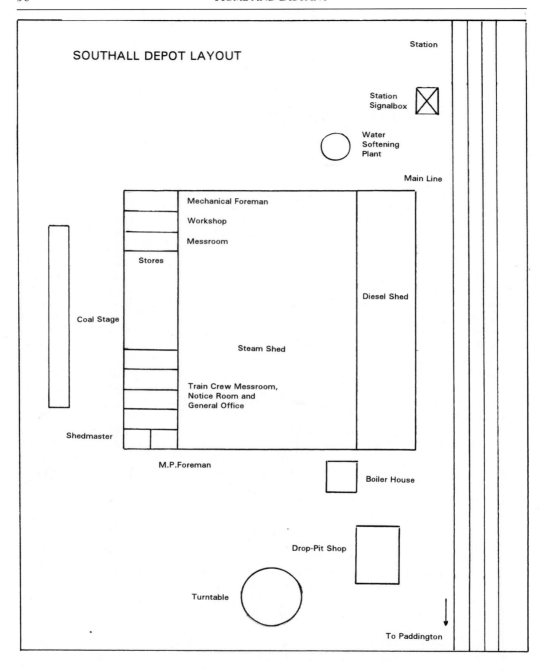

SOUTHALL DEPOT LAYOUT

Station

Station
Signalbox

Water
Softening
Plant

Main Line

Mechanical Foreman

Workshop

Messroom

Stores

Diesel Shed

Coal Stage

Steam Shed

Train Crew Messroom,
Notice Room and
General Office

Shedmaster

M.P.Foreman

Boiler House

Drop-Pit Shop

Turntable

To Paddington

Above right Driver D. Ritchings turns 2-6-2T No 6106 on the turntable at Southall. *Middlesex County Times*

Right Since preserved, No 6106 is seen in its new home at the Great Western Society's Didcot shed. *Author*

way to Southall. After a general discussion on the depot, Peter Sutton left us and I was introduced to many of the supervisory and clerical staff. The chief clerk, Gordon Collins, was to remain a close family friend for many years until his sudden death in 1974. The mechanical foreman was Maurice Blewett, whom I had first met at the interviews for the shedmaster's position less than a week previously. I was later to learn from Maurice that I was the first shedmaster at Southall to be appointed from the maintenance side. All previous appointments had been filled by people who had commenced their railway career in the train crew grades. This had been standard Western Region practice, but now the WR was coming into line with the other BR regions.

As with any job that involves being away from home, the question of lodgings was once again at the front of my mind. I knew that, in common with many WR depots, Southall had a hostel, and while these had originally been built to accommodate train crews working 'double home' duties, I anticipated that I could stay there at least until I could find something more permanent. During a discussion with the chief clerk, he mentioned that Ted Taylor, one of the shed drivers, was often willing to take in lodgers. Fortunately Ted was on duty and agreed that I could stay with him and his wife. This proved to be another home where I was treated as one of the family and I shall always

remember the satisfying breakfasts prepared for me before I made the 10-minute walk to the depot. I thought my stay with them would be for about three months, but it eventually stretched to 11 due to problems in selling my house in Dover.

At Dover I had no responsibility for steam-operated services, but at Southall I was responsible for the maintenance of a fleet of steam locomotives that were not in the best condition. There were also DMUs, including single power cars, drive-end trailers, three-car units and two parcels railcars, together with a small number of 350hp 08 Class diesel-electric shunting locomotives. The steam fleet included locomotives from classes '28XX', '38XX', '4073', '45XX', '49XX', '57XX', '61XX' and '78XX', which worked local freight services to Acton Yard, Brentford Dock, Slough, Reading, Didcot, Oxford and High Wycombe via Maidenhead. They also handled inter-divisional/regional services to Swindon, Westbury, Banbury and a double home working to Severn Tunnel Junction. Southall provided the pilot locomotive for shunting duties at High Wycombe, and two of the regular locomotives on this duty were Nos 6106 and 5531. Many of the inter-regional freight services from Banbury were worked by London Midland Region Class '8F' locomotives, which were in much the same mechanical condition as those based at Southall and subject to failure and replacement by a WR locomotive.

Above left **Fitter's Assistant Ken Lewis works on a steam locomotive at Southall.** *Middlesex County Times*

Left **Work on piston valves in the drop-pit shop at Southall. Note the poor condition of the locomotive as the end of steam approaches.** *Middlesex County Times*

Right **The Southall group at the Reading Divisional Office dinner in March 1966. From left to right are Mrs Collins, my wife and myself, Mrs Blewett, Chief Clerk Gordon Collins (standing) and Mechanical Foreman Maurice Blewett.** *Author's collection*

In addition to problems with the mechanical condition of the steam locomotives, services were also being cancelled due to a shortage of firemen. Eventually this was solved by importing firemen from the Scottish Region where steam traction was being phased out. The timekeeping of certain train crew staff, especially when they were rostered on duties commencing between midnight and 6.00am, was a continual problem for the motive power foremen. Eventually I had to dismiss one driver whose persistent absences caused the regular cancellation of a number of freight services.

Again unlike Dover, where I was responsible to a Motive Power Officer who had overall responsibility for maintenance staff and train crews, at Southall I was responsible to two people in the Divisional Office at Paddington. For all issues concerning maintenance staff and standards I reported to the Divisional Maintenance Engineer, but train crew matters at Divisional level came under Fred Brookes, the Traction & Train Crew Officer. I first met Fred ('Notcher') Brookes at the interview for the Southall job. He became a regular, almost weekly, visitor to Southall depot and gave me a lot of career guidance. Although a fairly recent WR arrival, he quickly got his nickname as a result of insisting that drivers used the full throttle position on the 'Warship' Class diesel-hydraulic locomotives to improve punctuality.

One afternoon, returning from a meeting at Reading, Fred and I travelled in the cab of the locomotive and were almost involved in a 'signal passed at danger' incident. At Ealing Broadway, where the maximum line speed decreased from 90 mph to 75 mph, the driver shut off power and allowed the train to 'coast' to lose speed. On passing Friars Junction the driver then saw that we were approaching caution signals and applied the brake, but I am sure we would not have stopped in time if the red stop signal at Old Oak Common had not changed to caution as we approached it.

Fred Brookes was very progressive in his outlook, and during the two years that I was at Southall we introduced a depot expenditure budget for all staff. This was a very laborious task as it meant costing every turn of duty at the depot, then assessing the depot costs for individual groups of staff weekly. The way that we did this budget was not as sophisticated as later budgets were to prove, but at least we had a rough assessment of the costs of the depot. In the mid-1950s railway costs came under very close scrutiny with the appointment of Divisional Traffic Costing Officers, and some months after my first budget discussion with Fred Brookes I was called to a meeting with Divisional Manager David Pattisson and the station managers from West Ealing and High Wycombe. The subject for discussion was 'Expenditure Budgets' and the chairman explained that headquarters was now considering the merits of monitoring depot costs in this way. As I had already been involved in this for a few months he asked me to outline our system at Southall. The meeting did not last long but we could all see that depot budgeting was on its way.

At Southall I had my first contact with staff who originated from the West Indies and West Africa. Most were from the former and were allocated to boiler-washing, coaling, fire-dropping, tube-cleaning and steam-raising duties. Apart from one individual, who was eventually dismissed, I found them very reliable workers. Although each man had specific duties it was quite common, at shift changeover times, to find them all working at the coal stage and later moving on as a team to the area where fire-dropping and tube-cleaning was carried out. This group of staff loved playing dominoes and I allowed this on the strict understanding that locomotives would not be delayed. In the two years I was at Southall I only had to remove the dominoes on one occasion!

Being interested in people's backgrounds I asked one of the fire-droppers, Ivan Rynd, why he came to England. He said that his sole reason was to get a regular job, explaining that in the West Indies occasional work was often available but there was no guarantee how long it would last. The only West African in the depot was Moses Ayetoso, a chargehand electrician in the diesel depot. He could be volatile at times but was very good at his work.

Staff relationships at Southall were very good. Out of the four members of the train crew LDC, one eventually joined the ASLEF

A hard steam working meant a lot
of ash to be cleared from the
smokebox, a job Southall's W.
Benjamin is pictured tackling.
Middlesex County Times

headquarters staff and another, the secretary, I
was subsequently to appoint to a position at
BRB headquarters.

While I had no specific on-call
responsibilities at Southall I did go out with the
tool vans on a few occasions to derailments in
local yards. My office was next to that occupied
by the motive power foremen, and since the
drivers kept them supplied with tea I was
fortunate enough to get the same treatment.

During my period at Southall I witnessed
the early stages of the elimination of steam
traction from the London Division. When
Old Oak Common steam depot closed its
allocation of steam locomotives was
transferred to us. Some remained in service,
but the majority were placed in the sidings on
the south side of the depot to await transfer to
Barry in South Wales where they were to be

cut up for scrap. By the time I left at the end
of 1965 these sidings were almost full of steam
engines of various classes from 'Kings' to
'57XX' tanks. Most had been cannibalised to
keep other locomotives in working order, and
many had lost name and number plates to
souvenir-hunters.

As I had a long spell in lodgings I was able to
make full use of my footplate permit. I was able
to cover the whole of the London Division, and
on a few occasions I went as far as Swindon and
Banbury. Most of my trips were on steam
workings, but as more diesels arrived I was able
to gain experience with both diesel-electric and
diesel-hydraulic locomotives. One of my
favourite trips was to catch the 7.10pm steam-
hauled service from Paddington to Banbury,
returning about 30 minutes later on a service
from Wolverhampton. The latter was usually

hauled by a 2,750hp Sulzer-engined locomotive, which regularly attained 95mph on the descent from Beaconsfield through Gerrards Cross.

Staff shortages and steam locomotive failures were still a major problem at the time, and we began to experience a number of diesel failures. To overcome the latter the motive power foremen made a priority of always having two steam locomotives ready for service, one facing London and the other facing Reading. This was achieved by getting locomotives ready 6 or 7 hours before their next rostered working so that they could be called upon during that period if needed. It was surprising how often we had to use this facility to minimise delays. I recall one example when an up service failed in Southall station and we had to use a '61XX' steam locomotive to haul the train and the failed diesel on to Paddington.

There were plenty of incidents of various sorts during my time at Southall. One morning, while talking to the Divisional Locomotive Engineer, we heard from Control that an up diesel-hauled South Wales service had failed at Taplow with a brake defect and an assisting engine from Southall was needed. The Locomotive Engineer suggested that we should go to Taplow and try to ascertain the cause of the failure while awaiting the arrival of the assisting locomotive.

On arrival at Taplow we spoke to the driver of the failed train, who said that after passing Maidenhead he had noticed a complete loss of train pipe vacuum, which he had not been able to overcome. Asking him to place the brake valve in the running position, we began checking for leaks. Even before we reached the first coach we could hear the sound of air being drawn into the train pipe. On examination we found a hole in the metal pipe, behind the buffer beam and consistent with being hit by something very heavy. Further examination revealed that part of the AWS gear was missing.

This was not all. When the assisting locomotive arrived the complete train was brought into Taplow station to enable the passengers to detrain and continue their journey to Paddington. Arrangements had

also been made with the signalman to move the defective locomotive to the sidings and have the coaches taken to Paddington for their next working. However, as soon as the train moved we could hear the noise made by 'flats' on the wheel tyres.

It was clear that the full brake application had locked all the wheels and, instead of the coaches going to Paddington, they now had to be hauled very slowly to Old Oak Common for tyre turning.

While at Southall I was involved in another situation connected with tyre-turning. This was linked with arrangements made for the Eastern Region at Stratford to do the tyre-turning for any of our DMU units. One evening I decided to accompany one of the units on its journey to east London. As Southall drivers were not familiar with the route, an ER pilotman was rostered to join us at Acton Yard. We left there with the pilotman on board and were then stopped at Acton Wells Junction. When the pilotman went to the signal box to ascertain the reason he was advised that a freight train was having trouble climbing the bank to Kensal Green and required assistance. As it was only a light train we agreed to see if we could help. It was quite foggy and the signalman said that the guard of the freight train would be waiting for us by the protection detonators. We moved forward slowly, our senses alert for a hand signal or the noise of an exploding detonator. In fact the first thing we saw was the tail light on the brake-van and the first thing we heard was a voice saying, 'Gee, man, you've arrived'. Despite the conditions the guard had just not bothered to protect his train in accordance with the Rule Book!

A check with the guard revealed that the train was made up of 20 wagons and, after a consultation with the signalman, we agreed to assist it forward to Kensal Green Junction. We decided against coupling up as we thought that if the combined train was stopped for uncoupling the freight portion might not be able to start again. Once the signals were cleared our driver applied power and got the freight train on the move. It then gradually picked up speed and when we stopped at Kensal Green Junction box all we could see was its tail light disappearing into the distance.

Another interesting incident arose one lunchtime while I was discussing a problem with the motive power foreman. The Control office rang to say that the 'Pines Express' was being diverted via Southall and Greenford due to a derailment at Oxford and would require a fresh train crew from Southall to work it forward to Banbury. It was agreed that the only possible way of meeting this requirement would be to cancel the 1.10pm freight service to Swindon. I was still in the motive power foreman's office when the crew arrived for the Swindon service. On being advised of the altered working the driver, who was known for his awkwardness, asked what locomotive was on the train. When told that it was an unmodified Southern Region 'West Country' Class 4-6-2, he immediately declined the job on the grounds that he knew nothing about these locomotives. With no WR engine available due to previous failures I offered to go with the driver to give him any necessary guidance, since WR crews were not familiar with the steam reversing gear and rocking grates on the 'West Country' Class. After some thought he agreed.

When the train arrived at Southall the position was not very good. Boiler pressure was only about 160 psi and the water level in the boiler was less than halfway up the glass. While the initial part of the journey to Northolt Junction was over fairly level track, I knew that once we passed the junction there was a 10-mile climb to Beaconsfield ahead, so I advised the fireman to build up the fire and, without sacrificing steam pressure, I would try to increase the boiler water level. At the same time I gave the driver instructions on working the steam reversing gear. All went so well that by the time we passed Northolt Junction the pressure was up to 200 psi and the water level almost to the top of the gauge glass. We managed to maintain this situation for the rest of the journey to Banbury, where the driver commented favourably on the locomotive and expressed his thanks for the assistance I had given.

With the gradual increase in the number of privately owned steam locomotives running on BR, I was pleased to have LNER 'A3' Class 'Pacific' No 4472 *Flying Scotsman* at Southall on two occasions. On its first visit the locomotive was used in a commercial to advertise a car polish. Much to the delight of the staff a number of scantily clad young ladies were photographed applying a wax car polish to the boiler casing. Water was then sprayed on to the polished surface to demonstrate the water-repellant nature of the polish. When the owner asked me what I thought about the advertisement, I commented that the polish seemed pretty good but had he wondered where all the water had gone? He had not considered that with such large quantities of water involved some might get into the axleboxes. Fortunately for him and the locomotive we were able to drain the boxes and refill them with oil before the locomotive departed.

The reason for the second visit to Southall was an attempt to beat the official timing for a non-stop, steam-hauled run from Paddington to Cardiff. When the train crew diagrams for the service were issued they indicated that a Southall crew would prepare the locomotive and take it to Paddington where they would be relieved by an Old Oak Common crew. I immediately spoke to the diagram office and asked why a Southall crew could not work to Cardiff. They pointed out that normally through services were manned by staff with the appropriate route knowledge, and as Southall depot had no rostered work to Cardiff it would mean providing a pilotman, which they were not prepared to do. What they did not know was that I had an ex-Newport driver at Southall who still included Paddington-Cardiff on his route card. In these circumstances my views were accepted, and Southall's Driver Bob Williams worked the service although no records were broken as the locomotive failed at Swindon.

I saw the train pass through Tilehurst on the Saturday morning and noticed a very bad leakage of steam from the left-side piston valve. When I arrived at the depot on the following Monday my staff had already examined *Flying Scotsman* and had found that the nuts securing the back steam chest cover were all loose. The Regional Traction & Train Crew Officer telephoned me and said that he had heard from the owner, who was blaming Southall for the failure, even hinting

Left **An immaculate *Flying Scotsman* at Southall.** *Author*

Above ***Flying Scotsman* on its ill-fated run to Cardiff, but already leaking steam badly and eventually to fail at Swindon.** *Author*

that the locomotive had been sabotaged. I explained that as the locomotive had come direct from Doncaster Works we had only been required to carry out a normal 'daily' visual examination, and since the steam chest cover was out of sight behind a metal sheet staff would not have been able to see the nuts, let alone whether they were correctly tightened. I could have added that if I had wished to sabotage the locomotive I would have made a better job of it by loosening part of the motion for the inside cylinder, but perish the thought!

Another privately owned locomotive, ex-GWR 4-6-0 No 4079 *Pendennis Castle*, spent some time at Southall following its overhaul, and I had a number of trips on the footplate during its running-in period.

An incident that arose during the later part of my stay at Southall concerned the manning of special services. Every year a firm at High Wycombe hired three special trains for their annual staff outing, and the usual destinations were Bournemouth, Weymouth or Portsmouth. Aware of the rapid disappearance of steam, on this occasion they particularly requested steam haulage of their services. Three locomotives were selected for the special trains – No 7808 *Cookham Manor*, No 6998 *Burton Agnes Hall* and No 6959 *Peatling Hall* – and special efforts were made to ensure they were in a good mechanical condition.

When the diagrams were issued they showed that the trains would be operated under the 'short rest' arrangements whereby the train crew, with a pilotman, would work through to the destination, have their break, then return with the back working. Southall crews were diagrammed to prepare the locomotives, work the empty stock to High Wycombe, and then be relieved at Greenford by Old Oak Common crews. The route knowledge of my depot staff was equal to that of the Old Oak Common men, no one at either depot having signed for the route beyond Southcote Junction, and I again felt strongly that we should not be deprived of the best part of this interesting and out-of-the-ordinary working. It took a lot of argument with the diagram office, but eventually my view was accepted and Southall men worked the whole job.

The annual general meeting of the Talyllyn Railway Society had been planned for Cup Final day in 1965 and the society also made a request for steam haulage of its special train. No 4079 *Clun Castle* was allocated and the necessary preparations carried out. However, when I arrived at Southall on the Saturday morning I found that the locomotive had not left the depot and a quick chat with the motive power foreman revealed that it had failed due to a leaking joint in the smokebox. The fire had been removed and staff were trying to pin-point the exact location of the defect.

During the morning I had a call from

The first 'modified Hall', No 6959 *Peatling Hall*, since preserved. *Author*

Regional Traction & Train Crew Officer Bill Thorley requesting a special effort to repair the locomotive and get it to Crewe for the return working of the special train. I made no promises in view of the lure of the Cup Final that afternoon, but assured him that we would do our best. Later I was advised by the duty fitter that a joint on the steam pipe between the regulator and the steam chest had blown, but he firmly declined to work overtime to repair it. The rest of the maintenance staff felt the same.

I knew I could do the job myself, but not without assistance, and while I was considering the problem two of Southall's boiler-washers, Michael Duffy and Alfie Attz, came along and volunteered to help. Michael asked to go to the local pub first in order to sell his Cup Final tickets, and he returned with sandwiches and rolls for our lunch. By mid-afternoon the defective joint had been

replaced, the fire relit and steam pressure built up to permit a satisfactory steam test.

I telephoned Bill Thorley with the good news, thinking how nice it would be to go home and get cleaned up, but I was asked if I would travel with the locomotive to make sure it got to Crewe and back to Paddington without further difficulties. I could not resist this footplate trip and soon after 5 o'clock we were away from Southall with Driver Ivor Richards and his fireman and heading for Banbury via Oxford. At Banbury the Southall crew was relieved by another crew to take the locomotive on to Shrewsbury, where it was serviced and turned on the shed before continuing to Crewe. I manage to nip out to the local fish and chip shop while this was going on, as it was a long while since I had last eaten. We moved on from Shrewsbury with a real sense of personal achievement.

When the special from Talyllyn arrived at

No 7029 *Clun Castle* pictured at Southall ready to work the last steam-hauled train out of Paddington on 11 June 1965. *Author's collection*

Crewe the members of the Talyllyn Railway Society were clearly elated to find *Clun Castle* waiting for them. The journey back passed without incident, but I was glad to be home after being on duty for more than 28 hours. On the Monday there were appreciative telephone calls from the Divisional Manager and the Regional Traction & Train Crew Officer. Another reward came at the end of the month when I found that I had been paid for the whole period on duty.

During the early part of 1965 there were serious problems with the provision of steam locomotives to meet service requirements due to their poor mechanical condition. Many of these machines were in need of some form of classified repair and it was agreed that we could carry out selected jobs including the machining of cylinder liners and valve sleeves. However, due to limited space in the drop-pit shop, staff could only work on one locomotive at a time and until that was completed no other machining could be undertaken. During a discussion with the mechanical foreman on how to improve the locomotive throughput, we came up with the idea of stripping a locomotive outside the shop with staff in the shop reassembling the repaired locomotive. The only problem was our shortage of staff on steam locomotive repairs, so the originators of the idea finished up doing the work themselves! On one occasion, on a lovely sunny day, we had donned our boilersuits and were busy removing the motion from a 'Manor' Class locomotive when the Divisional Maintenance Engineer made an unannounced visit to the depot. On arriving and finding that I was not in my office, he enquired as to my whereabouts and was directed to the area in which we were working. On seeing what we were doing he commented that we were expected to manage the depot and were not employed for repair work. However, being aware of the current problems, he did thank us for our efforts! It made me wonder why shedmasters were provided with boilersuits and dustcoats if they were not expected to wear them.

Southall depot had always lived in the shadow of Old Oak Common and had been guided by the decisions made there. It was the only depot with which I have ever been involved where passed firemen were only allowed to sign their route cards for local yards. This seemed utterly ridiculous to me since passed firemen were normally employed on main-line services.

Due to an increase in the number of trains of petroleum products from the refineries at Thames Haven, we were offered, with only four weeks' notice, some regular workings from Thames Haven to Thame. In view of the importance of this additional work I discussed the matter with the train crew LDC and it was agreed to select Jim Newbury for the first services as he was very quick to learn new routes. Sure enough he signed his route card after four weeks and most of the other drivers met the same criterion.

The last timetabled, steam-hauled passenger train from Paddington was the 4.15pm service to Banbury on Friday 11 June 1965, and it was hauled by No 7029 *Clun Castle*. This ended a 127-year era that had begun on 4 June 1838 when *North Star*, an 18.75-ton broad gauge locomotive built by Robert Stephenson, had hauled a directors' special to Maidenhead. During the last week I managed to obtain a footplate permit for my brother and myself to ride with Charlie Dodderidge and *Clun Castle* on the historic trip.

Having been at Southall for almost two years I became aware of changes taking place in the management structure at motive power depots. The shedmaster at Old Oak Common had recently retired and his position had been taken over by an Area Maintenance Engineer, with an ex-footplateman being responsible for train crew staff. Talking with Fred Brookes, he thought that the position of shedmaster would soon be obsolete and advised that I should look towards the new traffic organisation, which was seeking professionally qualified engineers to assume responsibility for the complete range of maintenance functions. I accepted this advice and, although I only had technical qualifications, applied for the position of Area Maintenance Engineer at Oxford when it was advertised towards the end of 1965. This was my first and only application for promotion since arriving at Southall.

6
OXFORD AND READING

After an interview I was appointed to the newly created post of Area Maintenance Engineer at Oxford in November 1965, where I was responsible for all maintenance functions in an area that extended to Didcot, Abingdon, Morris Cowley, Witney, Bicester, Kingham, Bletchington and Chipping Norton. Although I had previous experience on the maintenance of steam and diesel locomotives, at Oxford my responsibilities were extended to embrace carriages, wagons, 'outdoor' machinery and road motor vehicles.

Carriage and wagon maintenance facilities existed at Oxford and Didcot, with examiners based at Didcot, Hinksey, Morris Cowley, Abingdon and Bletchington. Outdoor machinery staff were responsible for electrical and mechanical equipment, including station and signal box water supplies and lighting, platform barrows and the facilities at Oxford for loading coal on to locomotive tenders. Although Chipping Norton was no longer rail-connected, a water pumping system was still in use there and required regular servicing. The road motor engineer's staff, located in a fairly modern depot at the southern end of the station, carried out repairs and examinations on motor vans and articulated units and trailers allocated to the parcels and full-load depots, as well as to the Area Manager's car.

This was my first promotion that did not require a move of home. My new office was situated in the depot at the north end of the station where steam and diesel servicing and maintenance was undertaken. To assist me in managing the organisation I had Senior Running Foreman Joe Tretheway,

Mechanical Foreman Bill Miles and a small number of clerks. Supervisors Jones and Day were respectively responsible for maintaining the road motor fleet and the rolling-stock. One of my initial tasks was to progress the elimination of steam maintenance by the beginning of 1966.

Being a country depot Oxford did not suffer the same level of staff shortages as places like Southall and, in the main, staff were very reliable and co-operative. Due to the close proximity of the train crew depot at Didcot, considerable rivalry existed between the two places with the staff at both seeking every opportunity to extend their route knowledge in order to be in the best possible position to cover any additional workings that might arise.

Diesel-hauled passenger working by Oxford train crews took them to Paddington via Reading, Birmingham via Banbury and to Worcester over the old Oxford, Worcester & Wolverhampton line; there was also a small allocation of DMU work to Paddington. In my time at Oxford the line was still open between Kennington Junction and Princes Risborough, and I remember one occasion when the Paddington-Worcester services had to be routed over this line due to a derailment at Didcot.

The major freight activity in the Oxford area revolved around the motor industry and consisted of trains conveying components into the area from Swindon and block trains of completed motor vehicles from Morris Cowley and Abingdon to Scotland and to Dover or Parkeston Quay for export. On these latter services the workings were on an 'out and home' basis, with the Oxford train crews normally working to Acton Yard or Bletchley. The Bletchley trip was a fairly short one, but when a diesel-hydraulic locomotive was allocated the Oxford crew took on a pilotman at Bletchley and worked right through to Parkeston Quay. Once someone realised this, is was not long before the Oxford drivers were adding Parkeston Quay to their route cards to give them another profitable mileage turn and save the costs of a pilotman.

I had always accepted the fact that you do not apply for promotion until you have made a significant contribution in your current position, and I thus expected to remain at Oxford for at least two years. However, one morning during a routine walk around the depot I stopped to talk to 'Albert', who was responsible for cleaning the mess and locker rooms. He astonished me by predicting that my stay would not exceed six months and, when I mentioned the conversation to Joe Tretheway, he intrigued me further by saying that Albert seldom got things wrong. It appeared that Albert had a relative who worked in the General Manager's secretariat while he himself was always around to carry luggage when the Western Region Board members came down for meetings in the Randolph Hotel, and could have heard something on those occasions. However, I looked upon Albert's comments as merely idle chatter.

Road transport was not available at the depot but I borrowed the Area Manager's car when I wished to visit any of my out-station staff. This arrangement was very useful as I was often able to combine the Thursday 'pay-run' for Area Manager Bernard Whitehall with such visits. In a rural area like Oxford this pay-run involved driving over 100 miles in one day to locations as scattered as Morris Cowley, Kennington Junction, Charlbury, Kingham, Bletchington and Bicester.

Steam locomotives had first arrived at Oxford on 12 June 1844 when the line reached there from Didcot, and steam traction ended on 3 January 1966 when the last northbound steam-hauled 'Pines Express' left the station at 2.10pm. The locomotive, No 6998 *Burton Agnes Hall*, with Driver Faulkner

and Fireman Cook, had been examined and thoroughly cleaned before the Lord Mayor of Oxford, Alderman Mrs K. Lower, accompanied by Reggie Hanks, who had recently retired from the WR Board, drove it from the depot to the station. At the station the Lord Mayor, with a party of Divisional Officers and local BR representatives, gave the 'right away' signal for the train and No 6998 steamed away to close a chapter in Oxford's history.

Although my period at Oxford was short it was not without incident, including one in the winter of 1966 with a Blisworth to Reading parcels train. This was due to stop at Oxford for train crew relief purposes, but when the driver applied the automatic brake for the Oxford stop he noticed that the brakes were very slow to operate. Luckily the route had already been cleared so there was no risk of a collision.

The locomotive was removed from the train and hauled to the depot where examination revealed that water had collected in the brake system and frozen there, preventing the operation of the brakes on the train. Curiously I had never experienced this with steam locomotive braking systems, but the effect must have been similar to that of an unfitted freight train descending an incline with insufficient handbrakes pinned down.

While most of Oxford's main-line passenger and freight services were normally hauled by Type 3 or 4 diesel locomotives, the local freight trips to such places as Witney, Abingdon and Morris Cowley were usually operated by Type 2 D63XX diesel-hydraulic locomotives. One afternoon a message came in reporting that the locomotive of the Abingdon trip had failed in Abingdon station with defective reversing gear. The normal method of operation for this trip was that the locomotive conveyed a set of empty Carflat wagons to Abingdon, ran round them there, then placed them in the station for subsequent loading. The empty wagons left on the previous trip would, by this time, have been loaded ready for conveyance to Hinksey Yard where they would be formed into inter-regional freight services.

On this occasion the train had arrived at

Left No 6998 *Burton Agnes Hall* prior to departure from Oxford on 3 January 1966 with the Lord Mayor of Oxford, Fireman Cook and Reggie Hanks on the footplate. Below, left to right, are Divisional Manager David Pattisson, Shedmaster Joe Trethewey, Divisional Maintenance Engineer Bill Sidwell, Divisional Movements Manager Albert Barnes, and myself on the extreme right. *BR Western Region*

Below No 6998 pulls away from Oxford at the head of the last steam service, the northbound 'Pines Express'. *BR Western Region*

Abingdon without problems, but when the driver tried to reverse the locomotive to enable it to be uncoupled from the wagons, nothing happened. Although this was not a regular fault on these locomotives, it had happened before. Normally in such circumstances a replacement locomotive would have been sent out to haul the failed locomotive and train away. However, as Abingdon was at the end of a 2½-mile single-line branch from Radley, the fireman from the failed locomotive would have had to walk through to Radley with the single-line token before a replacement locomotive could enter the branch. Sending a fitter by road was another option, but the only one on duty was tied up with the failure of a main-line locomotive needed for an evening service. The only other option was for the mechanical foreman and myself to head for Abingdon and see what we could do.

When we got to Abingdon the driver tried once more to reverse the locomotive from the driving cab, but without success. Drivers trained on individual locomotive classes were issued with fault guides, but these only covered minor matters and by now maintenance staff were learning a few 'tricks of the trade', just as they had with steam locomotives. Accordingly the mechanical foreman and I went into the engine compartment with an iron bar, placed it in the appropriate position on the transmission box and pulled. After a few attempts this worked and we succeeded in reversing the locomotive. However, we did stay on at Abingdon until the shunting was finished and the locomotive had departed for Hinksey Yard with its train of loaded Carflats.

One Monday morning when I arrived at Oxford I was met by one of the motive power foremen who was quite concerned about something that had arisen the previous day. Apparently he had been walking round the depot when he saw someone looking at the locomotives. Quite rightly he immediately confronted the individual, knowing that no visit permits had been issued for that particular day. It turned out to be no less a person than the General Manager, but he did apologise for not making himself known to my foreman when he arrived and was probably pleased that he had been so vigilant.

When steam maintenance ended tenders were sought for the removal of scrap locomotive spares from the depot. The contract was eventually awarded to a firm from Bicester, but as road access to the depot was very poor we made arrangements for the scrap material to be loaded on to rail wagons and for these to be moved to a point where the contents could easily be transferred to a road vehicle. At the end of the clearance period I received an envelope containing £20 from the contractor, which made me realise how easily people could find themselves in awkward positions. I took the view that I had only been doing my job, promptly returned the money and made a point of making sure my Divisional Officer knew what had transpired.

In March 1966 I was called for an interview for a position on the Movements & Terminals Training Scheme. I learned later that my name had been put forward by Fred Brookes who had suggested to me at Southall that I should try to obtain a transfer to the traffic side of the organisation. I was successful in obtaining one of these training posts, based in the London Division, and I left Oxford in May – just as 'Albert' had predicted.

This training scheme, for which I was attached to the London Division, was designed to provide selected staff with a comprehensive knowledge of all aspects of railway operation at regional, divisional and local level. The London Division, which had over 50 stations and five major freight yards, extended from Paddington to Ardley (between Bicester North and Banbury), Bletchington on the Birmingham main line, Latchmere Junction (south of Kensington Olympia), Kingham on the Worcester line, Pewsey on the 'Berks & Hants' and Uffington on the original GWR main line to Swindon and Bristol. There were also branch lines to Abingdon, Bicester London Road, Brentford Dock, Henley-on-Thames, Maidenhead to High Wycombe and Marlow, Princes Risborough to Kennington Junction, to Staines, Uxbridge High Street and Uxbridge Vine Street, Windsor & Eton and to Witney.

The Division handled all the main-line expresses on the West of England, Bristol and South Wales lines plus those to Birmingham and Worcester/Hereford. It also had several important cross-country services and a busy pattern of commuter trains off the branches and along the main line to Paddington. Parcels traffic was heavy, especially at Paddington, Slough, Reading and Oxford, and there was a whole range of freight movements varying from the Oxford area car industry business to coal for concentration depots and cross-London transfers.

My training began in May 1966, and although up to two years was allowed for completion, in my case it was to take only just over one. During the programme trainees were given special projects and in some instances were used to cover vacancies in order to gain practical experience of various posts in the traffic organisation.

The initial stages of my training were spent at Reading General station working in the ticket and parcels offices. In the former I became familiar with the variety of tickets in use, in dealing with the public, with the daily and weekly balances of takings against sales, and with the accounts rendered at the end of each four-weekly accounting period. In the parcels office I again covered accounting procedures and also studied the Parcels Numerical Sorting System, which had been introduced to ensure parcels were despatched on the correct services. Before the scheme there was always a risk with staff whose geography was faulty that a parcel might be sent to the South Coast just because it had 'south' in the address, which caused no problem for Southampton traffic but meant serious delay for items to Southend or Southport!

I had not previously been confined to an office, and found that I could hardly wait for the next stage of training, which was to include station and freight yard operations. Once again I was to be involved in shift working, but then moved on to the Divisional Train Planning Office followed by a spell in the regional timing and diagramming office, where I was given my first project.

I was given the task of examining the distribution arrangements for the daily train working and train crew alteration notices, always an important and sizeable railway activity. Apparently Dennis Mann, in charge of the office, had heard about the recent innovation of fax machines – then in their infancy – and required an assessment of whether they would help in the dissemination of our notices. As a result I spent a day at a business efficiency exhibition at Kensington Olympia talking to representatives of firms manufacturing the new machines.

The problem was that at that time the machines were very slow. The average transmission time for one sheet of A4 paper was 5 minutes, and there were no machines that could send to a number of locations at the same time. While I believed that fax machines would eventually find their way into everyday railway life, I had to report back that they were not suitable for the required task at that time.

While I was in the Divisional Train Planning Office I was delegated to cover the position of a member of staff who was going into hospital for a short period, and spent a week with him learning the job. One aspect of it that I well remember was the Monday morning task of extracting and reporting to regional headquarters information from Control sheets on the timekeeping of the newspaper trains leaving Paddington on Saturday nights/Sunday mornings. I suggested that this was a complete waste of time as headquarters could get the information from their own Control office, but was told to apply the system. Although I covered the position for four weeks I never once supplied this information and it was never requested. When the person I was relieving returned to work he spotted the absence of file copies for my missing reports and, despite my explanation, later compiled and forwarded the information for the period he had been away. What a waste of time!

During my time with the Divisional Office the entire office activity was transferred from the rather drab accommodation in the Arrival Side Offices at Paddington to new premises in Western Tower, an office block opposite Reading General station. This move was generally welcomed by the staff, as many of them had their journey time reduced and the accommodation itself was much better.

Towards the end of 1966 I was asked to cover the position of the Traction & Train Crew Officer who was going into hospital for an operation. As this was the type of work in which I was particularly interested, I welcomed the opportunity. Only one thing springs to mind from this period and that is asking the Movements Manager whether he wanted to sign the letters I wrote in my temporary capacity. His forthright reply was that he was no expert on train crew matters and that if I did not have the courage of my convictions sufficient to sign a letter, then it should not have been written in the first place!

Early in 1967, during a routine meeting with Divisional Manager David Pattisson to discuss my training, he told me that I had been selected to lead the Cardiff divisional team on a study related to Surplus Track Subsidy. I welcomed this opportunity to get to know South Wales and to see some of its heavy freight movements such as the trains of iron ore being hauled from Port Talbot to Llanwern by three Type 3 locomotives. The team was to be based in Cardiff and would be examining the utilisation of all lines in the Cardiff Division, so once again I had to go into lodgings. However, once again I was fortunate and was able to stay with a cousin living in Williamstown in the Rhondda Valley.

On the first Monday morning I was briefed by Divisional Manager Albert Barnes, whom I had previously met in the London Division, and his planning officer, Reg Bryer. The objective of our project was to divide every route in the Division into sections between junctions as part of a nationwide exercise to examine the level of passenger and freight traffic to determine whether it could be concentrated on fewer routes and thus reduce the overall railway route mileage.

After this initial meeting I went over to Queen Street station, Cardiff, where an office had been provided, to meet the rest of the team. Apart from myself and a management trainee, the rest of the group was made up of displaced staff from within the Cardiff Division. Having local people on the team proved very useful as between them they had a fair knowledge of the train working in the Division.

The first six weeks of the project went well and we had already identified certain sections of line for possible closure, but then I was summoned to Reading for an interview with the London Divisional Manager. I went expecting it to be a routine talk about my training, but out of the blue came the

information that there was a vacancy for the position of Assistant to the Divisional Movements Manager at Reading and that I was being considered for it. I knew the previous occupant of the post had been appointed as Area Manager Kensington, but I did not know much about the job and getting it had been furthest from my mind.

However, a few days later I received a letter confirming the appointment and giving me a starting date. It also recorded the end of my training period and notified me that the Cardiff work would be taken over by the management trainee there.

While my training had brought me into contact with many of the sections of the Divisional Office, I had not been involved with the section that I took over in June 1967. My chief was Dick Kirkby, the Divisional Movements Manager, and he gave me a description of the duties of my new position. I was to be responsible for all Divisional operating budgets, the monitoring of works study schemes and for the examination of new proposals for alterations to track layouts in conjunction with new signalling schemes. I would also act as duty operating officer and be 'on call' every third week. Once again I was back in the real world of railway operations.

I was never involved in any major planning

Prime Minister Harold Wilson talks to Area Manager Hugh Jenkins and myself at Reading General station. *Reading Evening Post*

schemes, as these were carried out by the planning office, but I did have an input into the remodelling of the track layout at Southcote Junction and Reading New Junction. However, most of my time in the new position was spent on budgets and work study schemes, which I did not expect to cause me any major problems in view of my previous experience at Southall. Although I was on call I was only called out a few times and these occasions proved to be the most interesting part of my stay at Reading.

One evening the Control office rang to say that a DMU had been derailed at Ufton Crossing on the line between Reading and Newbury. On arrival at the scene I found that the train had hit a bull and that the dead animal was jammed under the leading bogie. This was clearly not going to be the easiest of matters to resolve. In the end we had to lift the unit so that a rope attached to a tractor could be placed around the bull's neck and the dead animal pulled clear. We then discovered that the impact of the collision had been so great that it had buckled the brake gear on the leading bogie and we had to remove this before the unit could be moved and normal working resumed.

On another occasion I was advised that a DMU had become derailed at the end of No 10 platform at Reading General, and immediately hurried over to the scene. The derailment had been caused by the driver moving his train before the signal had been cleared, and as a consequence the unit became derailed at the catch points. The Reading tool vans had been called out as there was no room to use a the crane because of the proximity of the station roof canopy. Divisional Locomotive Engineer Peter Sutton arrived soon after I did, and we agreed that we could undertake the re-railing without having to block the adjacent lines, much to the relief of the passenger movements people.

When the tool vans arrived we found that they had recently been equipped with MFD re-railing gear, which consisted of sets of hydraulic jacks and traversing equipment designed to raise the derailed vehicle, slew it back on its proper alignment, then lower it again. This was the first opportunity the

breakdown crew had had to try it out in a real derailment situation.

Although I had not used this latest MFD version, I had used very similar equipment when I was on the Southern Region. The only difference between the two types was that the SR equipment was quite heavy and relied on water as the hydraulic medium, whereas the newer version had jacks and traversing plates made of aluminium and used oil instead of water. As I had to explain the use of the equipment to the breakdown crew, the actual re-railing took longer than we would have liked, but eventually the job was successfully completed and the crew had gained some valuable experience in the process.

At busy times such as summer Saturdays and prior to Bank Holidays, when additional services were running, or at times when services were seriously disrupted by operating incidents, it was the practice for duty officers to spend time at stations in the Division to identify and help resolve operating problems and to comment on passenger utilisation of additional services. One recurring problem was that passengers seemed to be prepared to crowd on to regular services rather than take advantage of a relief service. The usual reasons given were that the relief followed the regular working and did not have buffet facilities. To overcome part of this problem arrangements were being made whereby the relief service preceded the regular train.

On the Thursday afternoon prior to the Easter Bank Holiday weekend I was delegated to keep an eye on the working at Reading General station, and while I was there happened to meet two old colleagues from the Southern Region, Motive Power Officer Stan Downes and his assistant Ken Gardner, who had been one of the shedmasters at Salisbury. During a friendly chat I asked if there was any possibility of obtaining a footplate permit for my brother and I to travel on a steam locomotive before they were finally withdrawn. The result was that the two of us had a very pleasant trip from Waterloo to Bournemouth and back. However, it was noticeable that the locomotives were in very poor mechanical condition and it was fortunate that they would only be in use for a

Above One of the Swindon-built 1958 'Warship' Class, D814 *Dragon*, waiting to leave Salisbury. *Author*

Below A view from the cab of D814. *Author*

Above Another 1958 Swindon 'Warship', D811 *Daring*, with its train at Exeter Central. *Author*

Below The view from the cab of D811 descending the bank between Exeter Central and St Davids stations. *Author*

further three months. A few months later I managed to get another cab pass for us to travel from Salisbury to Exeter and return on 'Warship' Class locomotives, quite a different experience.

The Thursday was also memorable for a sharp difference of opinion with the Deputy Area Manager at Reading. I had noticed that the main clock was showing the wrong time and that two other clocks were recording something different and pointed this out to him, expecting that he would put the matter right. I was a bit taken aback to be told that he was not having staff from the Divisional office telling him how to run his station! So much for teamwork.

One other incident during this period concerns a derailment on a Friday afternoon during the summer. It was caused by a broken rail at Charlton Mackrell and was, indirectly, to lead to my next promotion. The derailment, at this relatively remote spot, had blocked both running lines of the main route to Exeter. As a consequence wholesale diversions via Bath or Badminton and Bristol were necessary, which, in turn, led to major alterations to the pattern of services leaving and arriving at Paddington. I was sent to the busy terminus to assist the Station Manager and his staff in coping with the revisions. In fact, the Assistant Station Manager on duty and his supervisors had matters well in hand, so I put my efforts into helping with passenger enquiries, directing people to the right trains and advising them where to change for the less obvious places like Westbury and Castle Cary.

Services were still in a turmoil on the following Saturday and I found myself back at Paddington for a few more hours. This was, in fact, the first occasion on which I had worked at a major London terminal, which is a job quite unlike any other and one I found both interesting and rewarding, especially as it involved constant liaison with people like the motive power foremen, the reservation office staff and the assistant station managers.

There is nothing quite like a departure from the normal pattern of services to get the adrenalin going. Occasions like these render the normal stock and train crew diagrams almost meaningless, and everything, right down to revised seat reservations, has to be replanned on the spot, verified with those who have to carry out the new arrangements, then communicated to the passengers waiting to use them.

A few weeks after the incident at Charlton Mackrell I was called to see Divisional Passenger Trains Officer Paul Pearman. He revealed that I would be getting a telephone call summoning me to the Divisional Manager's office on the 7th floor during the course of the morning. I was, he said, to appear surprised, but then went on to give me the background to the summons. Apparently the Deputy Station Manager at Paddington had been promoted to a position at SR headquarters at Waterloo, and I was to be asked how I felt about going to Paddington to cover the vacancy. It seemed that Paddington Station Manager Charles Coxon had been pleased with my performance during the Charlton Mackrell incident and had suggested that I should be given this opportunity.

I think I conveyed suitable surprise at the interview with the Divisional Manager, and within a few weeks I had left the Divisional office on my way to a new phase of my career at Paddington.

7
PADDINGTON

Paddington Station Manager Charles Coxon was a highly respected person and one of a select few local managers allowed to continue the tradition of wearing a top hat and tails on special occasions. He was responsible for a large and important area stretching from Paddington to Old Oak Common West Junction, and had a staff of over 1,400 people in the operating and commercial functions. Most of the staff were based at either Paddington station or at Old Oak Common depot, with a small number at Lords Hill Yard, a small freight yard adjacent to Royal Oak Underground station. This yard dealt with wagons for the National Carriers depot at Paddington, for the Paddington full loads depot and for the 'missing goods' warehouse adjacent to Westbourne Park station.

One of the major changes of the period was the remodelling and resignalling scheme based on the new Old Oak Common panel box opened in 1967. When this came into operation many existing signal boxes were closed, including the former Paddington Arrival and Departure boxes. At the same time the track layout at the approach to the station was improved, making it possible for trains to depart from any platform without the need for special signalling arrangements. This, in turn, reduced the number of trains going to Old Oak Common for servicing and increased the proportion of turn-round workings into the station.

Although I was designated as the Deputy Station Manager I had my own specific responsibility for all matters associated with the station's extensive parcels business. This covered the performance of the up and down parcels offices, situated adjacent to platforms 12 and 1A respectively, and for the cartage staff who collected and delivered parcels and transferred them to other London terminals (and, following a reorganisation of the collection and delivery services, to High Wycombe). In addition to these specific responsibilities I was expected to have sufficient knowledge and expertise to deputise for the Station Manager and provide a management presence throughout the area.

Five Assistant Station Managers were responsible for the day-to-day operation of Paddington station. Three of them, Frank Hawkins, Horace Keeble and Howard Jeans, were on a regular shift pattern, with the other two, Nick Nicholson and Wally Richards, providing rest day relief and general purpose relief to ensure continuous coverage of the station activity. The three regular Assistant Station Managers also had individual responsibilities for staff rosters, the station working booklet and the bi-annual examination of staff in rules and regulations.

At Old Oak Common three yard managers were responsible for staff involved in the marshalling and cleaning of passengers stock, with an Assistant Manager Train Crews, Eddy Hayward, responsible for the train crews. Continuous supervision of the train crew depot was provided by the motive power foremen.

Commercial activities at Paddington were under the direct control of chief clerks, Willy Williams in the parcels office, John Humphries in the booking office, and Bill Jackson in the reservation office. All issues

Platform 1 at Paddington, showing the main station entrance, one of the great roof spans and the station clock. *Author*

involving commercial activities away from the station premises were taken care of by the Divisional Office. The Station Manager had his own personal clerk, who also looked after public correspondence and maintenance matters, with all personnel issues being the responsibility of the chief staff clerk.

On my first day at Paddington I was introduced to the duty Assistant Station Managers, the staff in the general office and to Willy Williams, who took me around his part of the organisation, explaining the workings of the two parcels offices and the cross-town parcels transfer arrangements. Parcels traffic arriving at Paddington by train was initially taken to the up parcels office where it was sorted into traffic for delivery and traffic for transfer to other London parcels offices for onward transit. Traffic for local delivery was then moved to the high-level office at the rear of St Mary's Hospital, where it was sorted into the appropriate delivery rounds. Parcels collected from the local area were brought into this high-level office and then either transferred to the down parcels office for onward rail transit or to the up parcels office for onward movement by cross-town cartage. All parcels coming in via the latter arrangement went to the down parcels office, where they were either loaded to rail or taken to the high-level office for delivery.

In our tour of the station I was amazed to find that it was possible to go from the down parcels office to other parts of the station through a labyrinth of tunnels running underneath the platforms. During renovation work on some of the platforms the contractors found traces of broad gauge track laid down during the last century.

While I knew a few of the senior staff in the Paddington organisation, I soon realised that there were a lot more I needed to meet if I was to continue my principle of being recognised when I was out and about in the area. Gradually I got to know more and more people, and by the time I left, at the end of 3½ years, I knew nearly everyone by name. Although I had no direct responsibility for the train crew staff, I always tried to travel with them in the cab when travelling between home and work.

On call responsibility was shared between the Station Manager and myself on an alternate-week basis, and I was fortunate to be called out no more than twice during my spell at Paddington. We also had an arrangement with the ASMs that made sure we received details of other incidents that did not require our attendance so that we were ready for any questions from the Divisional Officers.

Once I had gained an insight into the workings of the parcels offices at Paddington I began to see how problems had been dealt with in the past. In 1968 BR introduced 'Pay & Efficiency' proposals that were intended to reward staff for greater efficiency by improving utilisation and passing on some of the savings from reduced numbers. Paddington had a staff shortage and had got to the position where the establishment had been reduced but the savings had mostly been used for rostered overtime.

I emphasise that most of the staff were loyal and concerned about their public image, but there were others, including LDC members representing staff in the down parcels office and on the station, who were resolutely against any change that involved revised rosters or a reduction in overtime. This was despite the fact that considerable voluntary overtime was available on Saturday nights for handling and loading the Sunday newspapers. This subject gained emphasis at a meeting called by the Divisional Manager to consider improving staff versatility over the whole range of operating and terminal activities. Revisions to the Pay & Efficiency package had introduced the versatility element to utilise the quiet time that tended to exist in most job profiles, and the objective now was to take advantage of this and the new staff grading structure to revise out-of-date rosters and achieve a positive reduction in staff costs. Each local manager had the task of reviewing his own organisation and putting proposals for change and improvement to the appropriate LDC.

At Paddington we thought long and hard before putting any proposals forward, for we all knew that the outcome might be strike action initiated by the down parcels office, with the up parcels, the station, the guards and even the Old Oak Common conciliation staff following suit; the drivers and secondmen at Old Oak Common were expected to work normally. Despite these possible consequences something just had to be done to achieve more flexible and efficient working, and the Divisional Manager was confident of the backing of the Region's General Manager.

The obvious time to face any problems would be in January, when passenger and parcels traffic levels were normally low. Contingency plans were drawn up to cover the possibility of strike action and staff meetings then scheduled for early January. At the first meeting with the down parcels office staff representatives they contended that the existing staffing levels matched the workload and saw no need for any alterations. We tried a number of avenues in the search for progress or compromise, but certain members of the LDC just stuck to this basic attitude and the meetings got nowhere.

After three days I advised the staff representatives that, owing to their failure to discuss our proposals in any meaningful way, I could see no alternative but to go ahead with their implementation. While I had been chairing these meetings the Station Manager had been holding separate ones with the station staff and, unfortunately, he too had received a negative response.

On the day after my notification that the proposals were to be implemented the staff in both parcels offices went on strike and were quickly followed by the station staff. An immediate stop was placed on stations accepting parcels traffic via Paddington and a 'Warnpass' notice was issued for passengers travelling through the station.

Our contingency plans went into operation immediately and Locomotive Inspectors were brought to the station to carry out the duties normally undertaken by the shunters, which included the uncoupling of arriving locomotives and the coupling up of departing ones. During the course of the dispute, which lasted over two weeks, management staff covered many of the conciliation grade duties including shunting and carriage and station cleaning; a photograph of me, complete with my badge of office – a bowler hat – and driving a station sweeping machine appeared in a national daily newspaper.

Towards the end of the second week, just as some senior regional officers were beginning to get cold feet, we started to get signals that the staff were interested in returning to work and that the staff representatives were ready to give further consideration to our proposals. A further series of meetings was arranged at which our original proposals were accepted and the staff returned to work. While I have always been in favour of discussion and compromise I am sure that this dispute would not have arisen had there been effective management action earlier in order to prevent the situation drifting out of hand.

I well recall a particular comment made by the chairman of the station LDC, Charlie Mulholland, to the effect that they had been silly to go on strike as we had proved during the dispute that the shunting duties at the station could be carried out by even fewer staff than had been suggested in the management proposals!

Following the resolution of the dispute further proposals were placed before the down side parcels office LDC involving the reduction of the number of Sunday duty turns from 27 to seven. Once again the staff side were intransigent and at the end of the meeting I advised them that, since they were not prepared to compromise, I would make arrangements for the office to be closed on Sundays from two weeks hence.

The following day the staff side chairman went to see the Station Manager and suggested that the matter might be reconsidered if a further meeting was arranged. He was politely advised that they had had their time for discussion and that the statement I had made would be implemented. Happily, during the rest of my time at Paddington relationships with the staff representatives were quite reasonable.

While I enjoyed the meetings with staff representatives, there were other aspects of the working at a large station that gave me great satisfaction and I recall two particular incidents that arose when the Station Manager was on holiday.

I was in the office one morning when the Station Manager's clerk told me that a woman was in the outer office requesting to see me on a private matter. I agreed to see her and she was shown in. It soon became clear that she wanted to complain about the attitude of one of the sleeping car attendants. She stated that she had travelled on the sleeper service to Penzance during the previous week and alleged that someone had tried to get into her sleeping compartment. She also maintained that when she alighted the sleeping car attendant had pinched her bottom. I promised to investigate the complaint and to write to her when my enquiries were complete. She then said that her husband was a captain with the Blue Star Shipping Company and, since she did not wish him to learn of the incident, she would call to see me again when she passed through Paddington during the next two weeks.

I checked the rosters to identify the sleeping car attendant involved and then interviewed him. From my description he was able to recall the woman, but emphatically denied her allegations. By a curious coincidence the shipping company the complainant had mentioned was the one with which my father had worked, so I decided to ring one of its superintendents to see whether he knew of the woman's husband. To my great surprise I was told that no one of the name she gave was employed by Blue Star Line. Further investigation with the British Transport Police revealed that the address she had given me was fictitious. Suffice it to say that I never saw the woman again.

Staff shortages were a continuing problem at Paddington and managers and senior clerks were often used to cover vacancies in the booking office at peak periods. One Friday evening I was issuing tickets when a passenger requested a return ticket to a local station in Ireland. At busy times it was necessary to have a sailing ticket to board the ferry at Fishguard so I asked my prospective passenger whether he had one. When he gave a negative reply I suggested that there was little point in me selling him travel tickets as the next available boat with capacity available was not for another 48 hours. He continued to argue and then insisted on seeing the duty manager. At this point I picked up my bowler hat, told him I was the duty manager and assured him that my advice was correct. A little taken aback, he thanked me and left.

One of the most interesting aspects of working at a London terminal was the people one met. We had a system at Paddington that ensured that whenever Members of Parliament, ambassadors, royalty or other important people were travelling through the station their journey details were entered into the Station Manager's diary. Each morning I had a meeting with the Station Manager and one item always discussed was VIP travel. If the Royal Train was to be used, the Station Manager had to escort the member or members of the Royal Family from their cars to the train, which was always positioned on platform 1. A similar arrangement applied on the return. On these occasions everyone at the station always played their part in ensuring that everything ran smoothly.

The responsibility for other important passengers was shared between the Station Manager and myself. During my period at Paddington I had the pleasure of meeting members of the Royal Family who were travelling on normal services, three people who had held the position of Prime Minister, several cabinet ministers, ambassadors and various personalities from the world of films, television and sport. I had met Harold Wilson previously during a visit he made to Reading station, but at Paddington, where he was a regular user of sleeping car services, the meetings became more regular and I also got to know his wife quite well.

On one occasion I had to be at Paddington to meet Harold Wilson off the sleeper from Penzance, but found that, due to an urgent appointment, he had returned by air the previous evening. His accommodation had been taken by Elizabeth Taylor and Richard Burton, but they had left the train at Reading so these were two films stars I was not able to meet.

One interesting incident arose on a Saturday morning when the American Ambassador, Walter Annenberg, and his wife were travelling to Plymouth on the 'Cornish Riviera Express', due to depart at 10.30. When I met them at the front of the station the ambassador asked me if the train departure could be delayed as his wife had left some of her jewellery in the embassy. He also told me that they had contacted the embassy and arranged for the jewellery to be rushed to the station. After thinking about the matter I told the ambassador that I was prepared to hold the train for up to 10 minutes but no longer, as it had to leave before the Bristol service, which was due to stop at Reading, at 10.45. If this would not be enough I would arrange to have the jewellery sent on via the Area Manager at Plymouth. Having seen the ambassador and his wife on to the train I advised the driver, guard and signalman of the possible delay, the

former responding that provided he left before the Bristol service he anticipated no problem with timekeeping. As it turned out the train left only 8 minutes late and, having seen it away, I went back to my office.

About 11.30 I got a telephone call from the Divisional Chief Controller asking who had authorised the delay to the 'Cornish Riviera Express'. When I replied that it was my decision I was told that I could not take such decisions as this was an inter-divisional train and only headquarters Control could authorise such arrangements. In addition to believing that I had acted for the best, it was also clearly too late to change anything so I asked how late the train had been leaving the London Division. When he replied that it had passed the boundary on time I suggested that the matter had resolved itself and was not worth pursuing. I heard nothing more about it.

On one of the few occasions when I was called to Paddington during an 'on call' period it was to deal with a derailment that had blocked the entrance to four platforms. It had been caused by a misunderstanding between a shunter and a signalman resulting in a number of parcels vans being propelled into a platform that the shunter thought was empty but which already contained a number of vans. When I arrived at the station the Old Oak Common breakdown crew had already been summoned. An examination of the scene of the derailment quickly confirmed that we would not have any of the affected platforms available for dealing with trains during the morning rush hour. I agreed with the duty Station Manager's view that we should try to get the sleeping cars and other terminating trains out of the station as quickly as possible.

When the Old Oak Common panel box had been commissioned it had replaced a number of other signal boxes. Most had been demolished, but at Paddington, while all the signalling equipment had been removed from the Arrival and Departure boxes, the buildings had been left untouched. The old Arrival box at the country end of platform 10 provided an ideal vantage point for monitoring the station working. I was there about 8.30 and could see a passenger train standing at signal OOC57, which was the last

The old Arrival signal box at Paddington viewed from beneath the bridge carrying Bishops Bridge Road. *Author*

signal before the station. However, every platform in the station was occupied and it looked as if the arriving passengers would just have to wait.

Then I had an idea. I contacted the supervisor in the down parcels office and asked him to ensure that the deck area adjacent to platform 1a was clear of its normal parcels clutter and to delegate staff to guide passengers from the parcels office on to platform 1. I was aware that signal OOC57 normally gave drivers an indication of the platform into which they were being routed, but the facility did not include platform 1a since this was not normally used for passenger services. Having made my arrangements I got in touch with the supervisor at Old Oak Common box and asked him to contact the driver of the train involved and to advise him that his train would be going into the parcels platform. As the movement was taking place in daylight I could see no risks, as the driver would be able to see exactly where he was going.

After the backlog of trains had been cleared I went back to my office and soon heard from the Divisional Movements Manager who wanted to know who had authorised the unusual movement into platform 1a. His view was that such a movement was against the signalling regulations, although it would have been all right if we had used platform 12, the other parcels platform, as the driver would have got a proper platform indication in such a case. Unfortunately he overlooked the fact that platform 12 could only accommodate three or four vehicles and we were dealing with a 12-coach train. In the end we agreed to differ about the propriety of my actions, but they had worked and nothing more was ever said about my rather unconventional solution.

Christmas was always a very busy period at Paddington with additional passenger services running and the volume of parcels traffic rising dramatically in the weeks prior to the festivities. It was not unusual to have over 800 loaded 'BRUTES' (parcels trolleys) about, some of which just had to be stabled on the platforms prior to transfer to the parcels office. On one occasion I had a telephone call from Divisional Office asking why one particular BRUTE had not moved for 24 hours, not an experience I much liked, for I would have preferred whoever had seen this to have told me direct. However, we made sure that loads did not get out of turn by having the night duty staff put the most recent arrivals at the country end of the platforms.

Christmas was also raffle ticket time. Everyone seems to enjoy the opportunity to support a good cause and the possibility of winning a prize. Salisbury Football Club did quite well, for I was able to sell over 1,500 of their tickets in each of my years at Paddington. The staff there must have been quite lucky for I recall bringing many prizes back to the station after the draw. The station also did pretty well from gifts expressing the appreciation of firms and individuals.

Horace Keeble was responsible for the basic train operating and platforming arrangements. Assisted by Les Nulmyer, he produced the Paddington Station Working booklet, an essential publication showing the platforms allocated to inwards services, train formations, destinations and calling points. A similar document detailed locomotive working arrangements so that everyone involved knew what should be happening. However, there were many occasions when the basic programme had to be altered for events like special trains or trains conveying additional coaches.

One such instance concerned the 17.15 arrival from Bristol on Fridays, which regularly conveyed two additional coaches. The train was booked to be accommodated in platform 3 and its next working was the 18.45 service back to Bristol. In normal circumstances the train was routed into platform 3 via the up main line, but on Fridays it had to go via the down main line because of the extra two vehicles that would otherwise block the exit from platform 4 and delay the 18.30 to Plymouth. With most signalmen this caused no problems, but one man just could not seem to remember the alteration, even when he had been specifically reminded. In the end the signal box supervisor had to signal the train himself in order to overcome whatever mental blockage caused this peculiar situation.

After I had been at Paddington for about two years I became keen on having my own organisation where I could, once again, be in complete control. One week the position of Area Manager at Penzance was advertised, albeit the same grade as my own and only temporary. Having spent many holidays in the Penzance area I quite fancied a move to Cornwall and was confident that, even if the post was not perpetuated, I could always use my engineering background to get another job in the area.

In due course I was called for an interview, which, I felt, went well. A day later I met one of the interview panel on the station and was called to his office only to learn that, although I was the senior applicant, I would not be appointed as they did not want me to have to move twice in a short space of time.

In 1971, prior to his retirement, Mr Coxon bought a house in St Ives and moved there three months ahead of his actual retirement date. I covered his 'on call' responsibilities to allow him to go down at weekends. During this same period arrangements were introduced to strengthen the Paddington management structure. The Station Manager was designated Area Manager and my own position, although I was still deputy, was designated Assistant Area Manager (Operations). A new position of Assistant Area Manager (Commercial) was created and the first appointee was Derek Redmond. At Old Oak Common the yard manager positions were eliminated and Keith Eddy, with an increased supervisory staff, took over the responsibility for carriage marshalling and cleaning.

When the position of Area Manager, Paddington, was advertised I did not apply as it was graded MS5 and I was only MS2. The man who got the job had never worked at a major station in his fairly short career and it took him quite a while to get to grips with the operational complexities of his new job. I was quite apprehensive about working with him and an early confrontation rather confirmed this. After a period of leave I returned to take charge of the area as the new manager's leave followed mine. I found that he had left a letter instructing me to deal with a disciplinary case involving a shunter at Old Oak Common who had refused to carry out his supervisor's instructions. The disciplinary hearing had been arranged for the Wednesday following my return and it was quite clear from the letter that the punishment had already been

The farewell to Charles Coxon, Paddington's well-respected Station Manager, in December 1971. I can be seen in the right background of the photograph. *British Railways*

decided. Apparently the Area Manager had discussed the incident with Division, who had agreed to back his decision.

I had never prejudged punishment in a disciplinary case before and I was not about to change this practice, especially as I had known the shunter for some time and had always found him a reliable worker. At the hearing, where the shunter was represented by a member of the NUR executive, the charge was accepted but the representative made the point that it was a spur-of-the-moment lapse and that the supervisor's instructions had subsequently been carried out. I decided that as the shunter had been suspended since the incident this would be punishment enough, although it was not as severe as that proposed by my boss. My decision was accepted and no appeal against the punishment was made.

On his return from leave I gave the Area Manager a full account of what had happened together with a personal view about the

unreliability of relying on backing from higher places. He was not at all happy with what I had done, reiterated the contents of his letter, accused me of a bad decision and threatened to handle all future disciplinary cases himself. This never happened, of course, and the breach was healed by a later apology.

I was still anxious to get my own area and eventually my wish was granted. I was walking around the station one evening when Derek Redmond introduced me to Grant Woodruff, the Euston Divisional Manager. Our conversation touched upon my future and the fact that I had recently applied for the position of Area Manager at Cricklewood. Apparently the requirement there was for someone with an engineering background, to which I replied 'I'm your man', and was subsequently called for interview. The first interview covered a large number of applicants and narrowed the field down to two, myself and a colleague from Acton. I felt

My own farewell to Paddington.
Author's collection

fairly confident as my colleague had no engineering qualifications. The second interviews were conducted by the Divisional Manager and his Management Development Officer and involved a host of questions regarding the approach to the job as well as experience and qualifications. At the end I was asked if I had any questions. I just wanted to know how quickly a decision would be taken as I had a week's leave coming and could make an immediate start on looking for a house in the Cricklewood area.

That afternoon, not long after I got back to Paddington after the second interview, the Area Manager congratulated me on my appointment as the next Area Manager at Cricklewood. He had just heard the news from the General Manager, and when the Divisional Staff Officer gave me the same news later he was not entirely happy that it had already reached me informally. However, the fact was that I soon had written confirmation of my transfer to the London Midland Region in September 1972.

8
AREA MANAGER, CRICKLEWOOD

As Area Manager, Cricklewood, I was responsible for over 300 operating and technical staff in the Cricklewood area with a small number of technical staff at the outbased depot at Cambridge Street, near St Pancras. The majority of the technical staff were involved in the maintenance of Type 2 and Type 4 diesel-electric locomotives, 350hp shunting locomotives and two types of DMU. Four-car units with a power car at each end, each power car having two Rolls-Royce 238bhp engines, were used for local services between St Pancras and Bedford. Services over the old Tottenham & Hampstead Joint line between Kentish Town and Barking and three peak-hour services into and out of Moorgate were operated by 150bhp units fitted with trip-cock gear.

The pattern adopted by the Western Region of having local maintenance and operating functions controlled by separate managers was not used on the London Midland Region. In the London Division, Area Managers were located at Euston, Willesden, Bletchley, Rugby, St Pancras, Cricklewood and Luton, and each manager had a joint responsibility for the two functions. As I will make clear later, this did not create an ideal working relationship with the Divisional Officers.

My area of responsibility covered the whole mix of railway locations on the Midland main line immediately outside St Pancras. It extended from the north end of Belsize Tunnel to the north end of Elstree Tunnel and to Acton Canal Wharf signal box on the branch line to Willesden and Acton Yard. Both tunnels had twin bores each containing an up and down line, although in Belsize Tunnel the lines through the west-side tunnel were operated under Permissive Block, which precluded their use by passenger trains unless Absolute Block had first been introduced.

Signal boxes in the area were located at Finchley Road, West Hampstead, Watling Street Junction, Cricklewood Junction, Brent Junction No 1 and No 2, Silkstream Junction and Hendon on the main line, and Dudding Hill Junction, Neasden Junction and Acton Canal Wharf on the Acton branch. Finchley Road signal box, which controlled trains entering Belsize Tunnels from the north, had a feature that I had never come across elsewhere. Passenger trains on the converging up local and up main lines were directed to the east-side tunnel. For regulation purposes, when the 'Train Entering Section' telegraph bell signal was sent from Elstree to Hendon for a Class 1 train on the up main line, a bell rang in Finchley Road box advising the signalman that the train would be passing his box in approximately 6 minutes.

The maintenance facilities at Cricklewood, where fuelling, repairs and examinations were carried out, were in a reasonable condition, but those for coaching stock maintenance and cleaning badly needed repair and renovation. To minimise the light running of locomotives between St Pancras and Cricklewood, a fuelling point, with staff able to carry out 'A' examinations, was provided at Cambridge Street on the up side approach to St Pancras station.

So far as coaching stock was concerned, most of the coaches passing through the depot for daily servicing were allocated to other

Cricklewood Junction looking north during engineering work in 1977. The Acton branch swings off to the left, while the maintenance depot was off to the right beyond the signal box. In the distance are the yards stretching towards Brent Junctions. *W. Adams*

Finchley Road, looking south towards Belsize Tunnels in 1974. The slow lines are on the right. *W. Adams*

Looking towards Cricklewood station from a southbound DMU in 1977. Beyond the main and goods lines are the Empty Wagon Sidings and South Sidings. The northbound chord of the triangular junction with the Acton line can be seen rising from a cutting on the right. On the extreme right is the sight of the former Cricklewood steam shed. *W. Adams*

depots for their routine examinations, although Cricklewood did the examinations on two sets of coaches working the weekday 'Thames-Clyde Express', one Bedford to St Pancras commuter train and a spare set of vehicles used for a Sunday evening service to Sheffield. In addition, maintenance was carried out on vans used for a daily local newspaper train that served St Albans, Luton and Bedford.

The Cricklewood freight yard was on the opposite side of the running lines from the maintenance depot and consisted of two sections, Empty Wagon Sidings and South Sidings. The former comprised 38 sidings of which all but one was double-ended, and these were used to marshall inwards loaded wagons for local destinations and empty wagons for Leicester and Toton. The lone single-ended siding was reserved for wagons being maintained by Gloucester Carriage & Wagon Company staff. Northbound inter-regional freight trains awaiting train crews were usually held in the Empty Wagon Sidings, while those in the opposite direction were stabled in South Sidings. Local freight trips, hauled by 350hp diesel shunters, operated on a daily basis to West Hampstead, Hendon and Neasden.

Commercial responsibilities in the area were minimal and embraced the sale of passenger tickets at West Hampstead, Cricklewood, Hendon and Mill Hill Broadway stations and a few parcels at Cricklewood and Mill Hill Broadway. Clerical staff were based at these two stations, but ticket sales at the other two were handled competently by conciliation staff. A senior clerk, Arthur Webb, based at Cricklewood, was responsible for the compilation of the area revenue account.

Most of the drivers were involved with the operation of the DMU services between St Pancras and Bedford and Kentish Town and Barking, but to maintain traction and route knowledge there were a number of freight turns to Leicester, Nottingham, Derby and Langley on the Western Region. The length limit on freight trains to Toton was 100 Standard Length Units (SLUs). In my time at Cricklewood the maximum achieved was 97

SLUs, and it was quite a sight to see a train over 2,000 feet long departing from the sidings.

Most of the freight trains passing through Cricklewood conveyed either petroleum products from Immingham or Thames Haven or coal from Bettshanger Colliery in Kent or from collieries around Toton. To balance the inter-regional working by SR crews of trains into the LMR, Cricklewood men worked freight services to the cement works at Southfleet and Northfleet. Services to the former were hauled by a Type 4 locomotive and conveyed traffic in 16-tonne mineral wagons with a total train weight of up to 1,000 tonnes. The Northfleet traffic, from collieries in the South Yorkshire and Nottinghamshire area, was conveyed in 43 HAA coal wagons, each with a gross weight of 47 tonnes to give a train weight of 2,000 tonnes and was hauled by a Type 4 Toton locomotive.

To enable the Northfleet services to overcome the gradients en route, an assisting locomotive was added at Cricklewood. One of the train locomotives had to be fitted with a slow-speed device to enable it to proceed through the discharge point at Northfleet at the right discharge speed. I travelled with these trains on a number of occasions and found it a great thrill to be on the SR's South Eastern Division once again.

The Cricklewood Area Manager's office was adjacent to the administration block at the south end of the depot. Looking out of my office window I could see the arrival and departure roads, the carriage sidings and a short siding where rail tank cars containing oil for the depot heating system were discharged. One night when the tank cars were being placed in this siding the driver had difficulty in stopping the locomotive with the result that one tank hit the buffer stops and knocked them through the wall of my office! Fortunately no one was injured.

As this was my first appointment on the LMR I did not expect to know any of the staff in the area, although I had met a mechanical foreman from Cricklewood many years previously at a diesel course at Derby. I soon found out that Alf Edwards was still working at the depot along with one of the fitters displaced by the Bricklayers Arms closure.

On the first morning of my transfer to the LMR I reported to the Divisional Office at Eversholt Street, Euston, where I had a short discussion with Divisional Maintenance Engineer John Marston before going to Cricklewood with the Divisional Carriage & Wagon engineer. At the depot I met the Assistant Area Managers for operations, Jack Southam, and for technical matters, Jim Groom, as well as the chief clerk, Ted Alcock. I was then left to obtain my own insight into my new empire.

At the interview I had been told that there was no 'on call'. When I asked Jack Southam how such duties were covered he explained that initial calls went to the Area Inspectors at St Pancras and Cricklewood and that if they thought that a more senior person was required one of the two of us would be contacted. So much for me thinking that I was going to have a spell without on call responsibilities!

After I had been in my new post about a fortnight I was called to a meeting with the Divisional Maintenance Engineer to discuss my initial thoughts on the organisation and the desirability of any changes. It was there that I learned of the plans to electrify the lines between St Pancras and Bedford and to replace steam heating with electric heating on the main-line services to Derby, Nottingham and Sheffield.

I thought that the introduction of electric train heating would be a lever to enable me to get some improvements carried out in the carriage sidings, but there was said to be no money available for improvements apart from the installation of an electrical supply to enable coaches to be preheated. With hindsight even this proved unnecessary as locomotive-hauled trains were soon replaced by InterCity 125 High Speed Trains.

It was very difficult to recruit technically qualified staff at Cricklewood, and many of the people employed there had to travel quite a distance to get to work. Some of the staff lived in the Luton and Bedford areas, while one fitter, whom I had first met at Bricklayers Arms, travelled from North Kent. In view of these staffing difficulties I felt that any new depot should be sited at Bedford, but this view

was not accepted as the plans had already been drawn up for the Cricklewood alterations. Another factor influencing my view was that the provision of new facilities at Bedford might help eliminate the strikes amongst the maintenance staff at Cricklewood depot, which had a history of short strikes over trivial matters. These usually involved only the staff working the day shift; those on the permanent night shift normally came to work. The supervisory staff also worked normally and ensured that we were able to provide the required service.

The Divisional Maintenance Engineer made it quite clear that one of my priorities was to eliminate these strikes and the practice of getting staff back to work by paying them for the period on strike. All this came up at my meeting at Divisional Office, and I made a point of discussing it with my technical assistant when I got back. To my surprise he believed that the strikes had been condoned in the past, presumably rather than face up to the broader issues of the local labour market.

I had not been at Cricklewood long when matters came to a head. I received a telephone call one Sunday morning from the duty mechanical foreman to say that the maintenance staff had walked out in a dispute involving two of their number. Having checked that the full passenger service could be provided on the Monday I saw no reason to go charging off to the depot.

The background to this matter involved an effort to persuade staff to work overtime at weekends by arranging the rosters so that they worked Saturday and Sunday on alternate weeks, thus giving them one long weekend off in every two. All that happened was that at first men would not come to work on the Saturday but turned up on the Sunday when double-time pay rates applied. To overcome this an agreement had been made between the staff representatives and the previous Area Manager that anyone who failed to work on the Saturday without a valid reason would not be allowed to take duty on the Sunday.

On the Saturday before the dispute two men had been absent and only one contacted the depot to report that he was unwell. The foreman had therefore correctly implemented the agreement on the Sunday – when both turned up – by allowing one man to take duty and sending the other home. For some reason the staff representatives felt this to be wrong and, when the foreman refused to alter his decision, the staff walked out.

On the Monday morning all staff were working normally and the staff representatives were waiting to see me when I arrived about 08.30. I invited them in and asked what it was all about as I could see no logical reason for the walk-out. They explained that they had been hasty in their reaction to the foreman's decision and that if I would pay the staff for the Sunday turn there would be no repetition.

I made it quite clear that, since everyone was fully aware of the agreement, I would not pay people for time they had not worked. In effect this meant that the staff would forfeit 12½ hours' pay. A long discussion followed with the staff representatives, who said that they had always been paid in the past and threatened to call the whole of the maintenance staff out on strike. I stuck to my view that the action had been in breach of a proper and well-understood agreement, and this was to pay dividends eventually. I have no idea what went on at the discussion between the staff representatives and their colleagues, but they eventually came back and said that they were prepared to accept my ruling. From that time on I only had one other dispute during my period at Cricklewood.

Industrial disputes were not the sole prerogative of the maintenance staff. About the same time ASLEF, who represented the drivers and secondmen, were involved in a dispute with BR and were operating a campaign of working to rule. The Cricklewood drivers fell into three categories, those who carried out their duties normally, those who made a token response to the campaign, and those who would find any reason they could to make sure a train was cancelled. One soon learned which drivers fell into this last category, and if any of them were rostered to take a locomotive or unit out of the depot the motive power foremen made sure that, wherever possible, the workings were amended and involved relieving a train in service instead.

Being based in an area where there were many Irish residents it was only natural that the depot would be a target for hoax bomb scares. In one particular incident a telephone call had been received saying that a bomb had been left in the depot, and the British Transport Police were quickly on the scene. It was the normal practice to then check all motor vehicles on site to ascertain their ownership by referring to a register maintained by the chief clerk, which showed all parking permits issued and the registration number of the vehicle involved.

On this particular occasion only one vehicle could not be identified, and that had some sinister-looking cardboard boxes on the rear seat. A police check showed it as belonging to a person, not one of our staff, who lived in the Cricklewood area. The situation looked quite serious at this point. As a next step the police decided to investigate the interior of the car and broke a window to obtain entry. Just after they had done so along came a guard who saw the damage to the car in which he had arrived and was less than happy about the situation. He threatened to sue, but when the police pointed out that the car was not registered in his name and that it had a number of defects he decided to let the matter drop!

In my period at Cricklewood I had many disciplinary cases to deal with and in instances involving footplate staff the person concerned nearly always wanted to be represented by a member of ASLEF, usually the local organiser. I found the latter to be very fair and only once was my punishment altered on appeal. This particular incident concerned a driver who was found to be under the influence of alcohol while on duty. In view of the seriousness of the offence, at the end of the hearing I decided that the punishment should be dismissal from the service. When the appeal was held the Divisional Officer decided, partly because the driver and his family were living in a railway-owned house, that he should be suspended for seven days and taken off driving duties permanently.

In another incident a driver was charged with being missing from the depot during a night turn of duty. There was no doubt that he arrived for duty at 22.00 hours, but when the motive power foreman looked for him at about 01.00 he was nowhere to be found, although he subsequently booked off duty at the end of the shift at 06.00. The driver's response to the disciplinary charge was a complete denial of being missing and a request for a personal interview, with ASLEF representation. He also asked to call another driver as a witness to his presence at the depot, although this man had been involved in the search for the missing driver. At the interview I was requested to withdraw the charge, the driver being quite adamant that he had been on duty although he would not reveal his whereabouts at the time of the search.

When I suggested that we should call in the witness, the ASLEF representative requested a short adjournment, to which I agreed. Then, immediately the interview was reconvened, the driver's representative said that they accepted the charge as correct and would accept the punishment I awarded. I later found out that the driver had gone to the local Staff Association club soon after arriving for duty, and I also learned that in addition to my punishment he got a serious admonition from his union representative. My uncle, who acted as a representative on many occasions, had had a similar case where a fireman at Nine Elms protested that a timekeeping charge he faced was the first one when, in fact, he had already been suspended for frequent bad timekeeping.

At Cricklewood I had to discipline a supervisor for the first and only occasion. In the light of the high value of the spares in the depot stores, a previous Area Manager had decided that proper control demanded a high level of supervision and had appointed a supervisor for this purpose. Before I arrived the supervisor concerned had already been warned about his performance when a wagonload of spares had arrived at Derby contaminated with sand that had not been cleared out before the wagon was loaded. A similar incident occurred again a few months after my arrival, and, by means of the disciplinary procedure, I transferred the man to another post.

Not surprisingly, for Cricklewood was an important and busy depot, quite a few incidents occurred during my time there. One day I was in my office when there was a report that a passenger train from Sheffield had been stopped at the station because a signalman had noticed that a door was open. A passenger had also reported that someone had fallen from the train between Elstree and Cricklewood. All trains were diverted on to the slow lines and the District Inspector and myself decided to travel in the cab of a northbound service to try to obtain more information. We saw nothing on the journey from Cricklewood and decided to alight at the south end of Elstree Tunnel and make our way through the fast line tunnel on foot.

About 10 yards from the north end of the tunnel we found the body of a teenager. This was the first time I had attended an incident where a fatality was involved, but it was made a little less harrowing by the fact that the boy must have died from impact with the ballast for there were few marks on the body, although we could see that he had lost one foot. It later transpired that the lad had been standing by the door of a coach when it opened and he had fallen out.

Another incident concerned my efforts to maintain a full passenger service at a time when no spare DMUs were available. The last service to leave the depot in the afternoon was programmed to be formed with two four-car units. It ran empty to St Pancras, made one journey to St Albans, then returned to the depot. On this particular afternoon one power car developed a fault and, rather than run the train with only one unit, which would have reduced passenger capacity by half, I decided to remove only the defective power car and one trailer vehicle. This arrangement maintained the ratio of one power car to each trailer vehicle and only reduced capacity by a quarter, but I came in for later criticism on the grounds that there would have been even greater problems if another power car had failed. Right or wrong, the fact was that the St Albans commuters fared better than they might otherwise have done!

By this time, 1973, the Rolls-Royce-powered DMUs at Cricklewood, which had been introduced in 1959, were very prone to mechanical failure. One of the main problems, caused by intensive use, was that the main

One of ageing Midland line DMUs calls at West Hampstead with a St Pancras-bound local service in 1974. *W. Adams*

frame members were bending when the units were fully loaded. This caused problems in opening the doors, and a decision was taken to strengthen the main frame members.

My homeward journey from Cricklewood involved a change of trains at St Albans. One evening as we were approaching that point I noticed a locomotive-hauled train standing at the Home signal on the down fast line. After alighting from my own train I learned from the station supervisor that the locomotive had failed.

I walked back to the failed locomotive to speak to the driver and find out what had happened. He told me that as he approached St Albans he had closed the power controller whereupon the diesel engine had stopped and would not restart. I suspected immediately that the 'engine overload' had tripped, and an examination proved me right. After resetting the overload the engine was restarted and the train moved into the station. The passengers were still on the train so it was decided to continue on to Bedford. At the driver's request I went with him, then returned with the empty stock to Harpenden, all without experiencing any further problems.

A breakdown train with a 75-tonne diesel crane was based at Cricklewood, but my area was geographically so small that I was only involved in two crane incidents – derailments near Silkstream Junction signal box and at West Ealing. Most derailments only involved wagons, so it was much quicker to re-rail using just the jacking equipment.

In the derailment at Silkstream Junction a fully-fitted freight train from Cricklewood to Tinsley had passed the Home signal at danger and been derailed at the following catch points. When I arrived at the scene I found that the leading bogie of the Type 4 locomotive was buried in soft earth and the first three wagons were derailed. I discussed the re-railing arrangements with the breakdown train supervisor, then decided to try to establish the cause of the mishap. Speaking to the driver I ascertained that the train had travelled on the goods line from Cricklewood sidings and he assured me that the necessary brake test had been carried out prior to departure. Beyond Hendon signal box the goods lines are on a rising gradient and are carried on a flyover over the main line to then join the slow lines on a falling gradient at Silkstream Junction box. The driver was adamant that the Silkstream Junction Distant signal, which was on the same post as the Hendon Starter, was in the 'off' position when he passed it. At that time the area still had mechanical signalling and most signals were still lit by oil lamps.

In view of the driver's statements I asked him to walk with me back to Hendon to check on the signal aspects while the local Signal & Telecommunications staff were carrying out their technical examinations. When we got to the signal post the Starting signal was at danger and the Distant in the caution position. Although the signal lights were not very bright they were definitely showing red and amber respectively. I then decided to check Hendon signal box to see whether any equipment malfunction had been found. At this point the driver still maintained that he had seen two green lights, so he came with me.

About halfway between the signal post and the signal box the driver turned round to have another look at the signal and immediately drew my attention to what appeared to be a red and a green light showing. With mechanical interlocking this combination should have been impossible, so my initial thoughts were that there had been an equipment malfunction. However, closer inspection revealed that there was a room in a block of flats behind the signals that had green curtains, and the light from this room was sufficient to overcome the amber lens in the signal spectacle and give the appearance of a green. As a result the driver was exonerated from blame for the derailment, and to prevent a recurrence a board was positioned behind the signals to screen out interference from the domestic lighting.

The derailment at West Ealing involved a passenger train from Paddington to Oxford. It occurred while I was travelling home from work and was the first one in which I had been involved where people had lost their lives. On arriving home I was advised by the Divisional Maintenance Engineer that the Cricklewood crane had been placed on standby for the derailment and, as I had only recently left the Western Region, he asked me to go with the breakdown crane if it was needed.

About 21.00 I received a telephone call advising me that the Cricklewood crane was needed, so I agreed to make my own way to West Ealing by road and meet the train there. Knowing the area from the past I managed to find the derailment quite easily, parking my car in a side street and making my way on foot to the site, where the Old Oak Common crane was already at work. At the site I found a 'Western' Class diesel-hydraulic locomotive lying on its side and a number of coaches in a similar position. Some coach bogies had been torn loose and embedded in other coaches contributing to the number of fatalities.

It was subsequently established that the locomotive battery box cover had become loose and had fallen on to the point motor for the points controlling the junction from the down main to the down relief lines. In falling on to the point motor the cover had bridged the two terminals, which had caused the points to move beneath the train. The result was that the locomotive and leading coaches were on the main line while the rear of the train was diverted to the relief line. Fortunately no other train was involved. Looking round the site to find the person in charge I met the WR Divisional Manager, Humphrey Todd, who seemed quite surprised to see me in view of the fact that I no longer worked for the WR. Explanation given, he indicated that the Cricklewood crane's task was to start the process of re-railing work from the London end of the site. By this time the Cricklewood crane had arrived and we commenced our task straight away. Most of the coaches at the rear of the train had remained upright so our work of lifting them and placing them back on the track was not too difficult.

When I was relieved the following morning I decided to check on the depot situation at Cricklewood on my way home. Arriving about 09.15 I was advised that the Divisional Operating Officer, Tom Brazier, wanted to speak to me. When I rang back his first remark was, 'This is a fine time to arrive for work.' No one had told him that I had spent the night working on the West Ealing mishap, despite the fact that this had been arranged at Divisional Office!

Another curious sequel was a subsequent telephone call from Divisional Office asking me if I knew anything of the whereabouts of the nameplate of No 1007 *Western Talisman*, the locomotive involved in the West Ealing derailment. Apparently there was an allegation that it had been removed by the Cricklewood breakdown gang. The whole thing was news to me, but I talked to the breakdown gang supervisor, then told him that I would be away from my office for about an hour. When I got back I found the nameplate in my office and it was subsequently returned to the locomotive.

With the continual turnover of footplate staff at Cricklewood I always made arrangements to see all new drivers when they arrived.

One notable disciplinary incident involved a driver who came to us from Watford. Prior to his interview I had obtained the his personal file and was amazed at the size of it. Closer examination revealed one of the longest disciplinary records I had ever seen. It appeared that he had had a number of final warnings about his conduct, but after each one had got away with a reprimand on the next occasion. When he came into my office and saw his file on my desk he was in no way abashed but commented that his father had told him that I would not tolerate unreliable people in my organisation. I had not connected the name with anyone in my travels, but it transpired that his father was a supervisor at Old Oak Common. Anyway, we had our discussion, which I concluded by leaving him in no doubt that he was fortunate still to be working in the industry.

It was not long after this that I received a complaint from a driver on the passenger yard pilot that when he arrived for work he found a house brick jammed in the dead man's treadle on the locomotive. He removed the brick but let me know of his discovery because its use thwarted the function of the treadle. A check on the roster then revealed that the ex-Watford driver had been working on the passenger pilot on the previous shift. He was on the same turn the following day so I arranged for the Locomotive Inspector to check the locomotive at the end of his shift. That examination revealed that a brick had once again been placed on the treadle. This was a blatant breach of safety rules and I decided to invoke the disciplinary arrangements. At the hearing the driver pleaded guilty to the charge on the Form 1 and I decided that, taking his previous record into account, he must be dismissed from the industry. I did, however, agree to his request to resign instead.

While Cricklewood depot had a bad reputation for disputes, it also had many good points. For example, Taffy Hughes, one of the drivers, arranged a raffle week after week the proceeds from which went to the Railway Orphanage. When talking to him one day he explained that his father had died when he was quite young, leaving his mother with a very hard time raising children in an era when there were no social support payments. Resulting from this he felt that he had to do all he could for other unfortunate children and his raffle was his way of achieving this aim.

During my time at Cricklewood I came across an instance of a man declining to apply for a supervisory position despite the fact that he was covering the vacancy. Peter Flanagan felt that he stood no chance of getting the job as he was only a senior railman at the time. In the event, when all the other applicants were interviewed, none proved suitable. I therefore arranged for the job to be re-advertised and told Flanagan that I wanted to see an application from him. He was the only new applicant, I appointed him as a yard supervisor and eventually he progressed to another supervisory position at St Pancras.

Early in 1974 there were proposals to separate local operating and maintenance responsibilities. Although I could be identified with the Area Maintenance Engineer's position at Cricklewood I did not want to return to a purely technical post, and decided to apply for operating positions elsewhere. I was interviewed for the post of Area Manager, Willesden, but declined the position because of a stipulation that the successful applicant should live on the line of route. To move just 12 miles to Hemel Hempstead seemed ridiculous.

My next interview was for the position of Area Manager designate at Shenfield, and the interview at Liverpool Street was conducted by Claude Hankins. My experience seemed to be taken for granted and the questions were more about the approach to the job. I was asked if I ever lost my temper and replied in the negative. I was then asked if I ever got frustrated and, if so, what I did about it. I replied that in such a case I would retire to my allotment – which seemed to meet with approval for I was appointed to the post.

Accommodation for the Shenfield position was not immediately available so I was transferred in April 1974 to relieve the occupant of the post of Area Manager at Southend, Derek Norcott, who had suffered a heart attack. His actual position was that of Area Manager at Broxbourne.

9

AREA MANAGER, SHENFIELD AND BROXBOURNE

The Area Manager at Southend was based at Southend Central station on the former London, Tilbury & Southend line, and also had responsibility for Southend Victoria and the section of the old Great Eastern line to Wickford plus the branch line to Burnham-on-Crouch. In the new organisation this latter part of the area would come under my control at Shenfield, leaving the whole of the former LT&S line from Shoeburyness to Fenchurch Street under the control of the Southend Area Manager.

During my short stay at Southend I was actively involved in filling vacancies in the Shenfield area, and when the position of administration assistant there was advertised I was sent details of the applicants to consider, with suggestions as to who should be interviewed. Having studied the list of applicants I considered that Ted Alcock, my chief clerk from Cricklewood, would be a strong contender. The Divisional Staff Officer at Liverpool Street was in favour of only interviewing the six senior applicants, and Ted was a fairly junior candidate, but at my insistence he was included. He compared favourably at the interviews and, with my preference accepted, the old partnership from Cricklewood looked set to continue. When Ted told his family about the new job they had some difficulty in understanding how going from chief clerk to administration assistant was a promotion.

After Derek Norcott, who lived in the Shenfield area, returned to work, he suffered further health problems and the medical officer suggested that he should reduce his daily travelling. As I was having difficulty in selling my house in Harpenden, Derek suggested that we should consider exchanging positions with him, Derek taking the Shenfield post and me taking his Broxbourne job. We put this suggestion to Roy Calvert, the Divisional Operating Manager, who agreed that, as both positions were of equal grading and provided the medical officer could see no problems with Derek's health, the exchange could take place. Thus on 12 August I moved to Broxbourne and Derek took over the Shenfield responsibilities. Unfortunately he had further trouble with his health and eventually had to give up the Shenfield job.

In 1971 a prototype Area Manager's organisation had been created at Broxbourne and, although some of the original management team had moved to other positions, the basic management structure had not changed. When I arrived the position was being covered by Len Robinson, who was waiting to take up the Area Manager's job at Southend Central. It was agreed that he would have one week with me before moving to Southend.

The Broxbourne area included 43 passenger stations and extended from Cambridge Heath to Elsenham on the Cambridge main line. It included the Southbury Loop and branches from Clapton Junction to Chingford, Coppermill Junction to Lea Bridge, Broxbourne Junction to Hertford East, and Bury Street Junction to Enfield Town. Electric multiple units, based at Ilford Car Sheds, where repairs, maintenance and heavy cleaning were carried out, were used to provide regular interval local

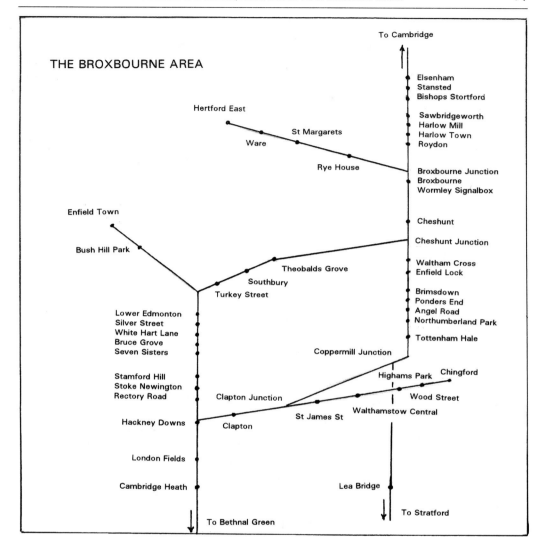

THE BROXBOURNE AREA

To Cambridge

Elsenham
Stansted
Bishops Stortford

Sawbridgeworth
Harlow Mill
Harlow Town
Roydon

Broxbourne Junction
Broxbourne
Wormley Signalbox

Cheshunt

Cheshunt Junction

Waltham Cross
Enfield Lock

Brimsdown
Ponders End
Angel Road
Northumberland Park

Tottenham Hale

Hertford East
St Margarets
Ware
Rye House

Enfield Town
Bush Hill Park

Theobalds Grove
Southbury
Turkey Street

Lower Edmonton
Silver Street
White Hart Lane
Bruce Grove
Seven Sisters

Coppermill Junction

Stamford Hill
Stoke Newington
Rectory Road

Highams Park   Chingford
Clapton Junction   Wood Street

Hackney Downs
Clapton
St James St
Walthamstow Central

London Fields

Cambridge Heath

Lea Bridge

To Bethnal Green   To Stratford

passenger services to Chingford, Enfield Town, Hertford East and Bishops Stortford, where daily cleaning of the units was scheduled.

Three services operated each hour to and from Chingford and Enfield Town, with two trains an hour to and from Bishops Stortford and Hertford East. The Bishops Stortford services were routed via the Southbury Loop and the Hertford East ones via the Lea Valley, with cross-platform connections provided at Broxbourne. Stansted and Elsenham were served by some main-line Liverpool Street-Cambridge trains and by the DMUs calling at all stations between Bishops Stortford and Cambridge. Most of the larger stations had facilities for Red Star parcels, with Harlow Town and Lea Bridge being the central points for 'collected and delivered' parcels. Cheshunt station had its own road vehicles for collecting the market garden produce traffic from the local nurseries and taking it to Lea Bridge.

The full loads depot at Harlow Mill handled general freight traffic and provided resources for shunting and placing wagons in the private siding of the United Glass factory.

Two traditional signal boxes in the Broxbourne area: Cheshunt (*left*), which controlled the junction between the Churchbury Loop and the Lea Valley main line, and, badly in need of a coat of paint, Hertford East (*middle left*). *Author*

Left Broxbourne station, with its modern signal box. *Author*

Above right St Margarets on the Hertford East branch, formerly the junction for the rural line to Buntingford. *Author*

Right Hertford East terminus, a station originally built by the Great Eastern Railway in 1888. *Author*

Single-commodity freight traffic was handled at the following locations:

Power station coal	Broxbourne and Brimsdown
House coal	Coal concentration depots at Broxbourne, Bishops Stortford and White Hart Lane
Bananas	Bishops Stortford
Heavy oil	Hertford East
Aviation fuel oil	Stansted
Scrap metal	Angel Road and Waltham Cross

All the administration matters for the staff establishment of some 700 people were located at Broxbourne itself. Due to the problems of obtaining suitable staff, there were usually about 70 vacancies, mostly in the area south of Broxbourne. The train crew depots at Enfield Town, Chingford, Hertford East and Bishops Stortford accounted for a large portion of the establishment. A train crew supervisor, Len Skeggs, located at Chingford station, and timekeepers at Hertford East, Enfield Town and Bishops Stortford assisted the Assistant Area Manager (Train Crews) in controlling the four depots. The second largest group of staff was employed in operating 17 signal boxes and 11 level crossings, with the rest of the area staff involved in station and terminal working for passenger, parcels and freight trains.

The management structure under the Area Manager consisted of an administration assistant, Chris Richardson, and three Assistant Area Managers responsible for Operating (Ken Green), Commercial (Don Harvey) and Train Crew (Bill Cleghorn). Bill Cleghorn and I had first met in my days on the SR South Eastern Division. Four outbased traffic assistants, two at Broxbourne and two at Tottenham Hale, were responsible for day-to-day operations in the area with assistance from supervisors at Tottenham Hale, Chingford, Enfield Town, Broxbourne, Harlow Mill Full Loads Depot and Bishops Stortford.

At one of the first Area Manager's meetings I attended the question of the competency of managers in rules and regulations was discussed. It appeared that the Eastern Region had adopted the practice previously applied with station masters and had always given Area Managers a bi-annual examination. I had never had to take this exam in previous managerial positions, but was told by the Divisional Operating Manager that I had better prepare myself. I was not too worried for I held certificates from various railway courses in rules and regulations.

As it turned out my examination lasted for over 6 hours, but only one problem arose and this concerned a specific bell code. I had never come across this as it was not in my instruction books, but the examiner was not satisfied with this explanation and produced his own copy. I noticed that the colour of the cover was slightly different and assumed that my copy must be an out-of-date version. The truth proved to be that the examiner's copy was the out-of-date one, and I passed the examination with no further problems! Having survived this initial gruelling scrutiny later examinations proved much simpler affairs.

The majority of the staff in the Broxbourne area were reliable, hard-working and co-operative. Such problems as there were arose in the southern part of the area where it was exceedingly difficult to fill vacancies. One reason was that people could not afford to live in the area due to the high cost of accommodation. As an example, one CO4 clerical position we advertised attracted only four applications, while a similarly graded position in the Manchester area produced more than 30.

In an attempt to do something about this situation it was decided to place a series of advertisements in local newspapers giving broad details of the vacancies that existed, the rates of pay and the fact that all jobs involved shift working. The initial response was good, with over 100 applications being received. These were examined and full information sent to the applicants we considered suitable for a vacant position. The next stage was to arrange interviews for those who replied, one of whom wrote that he was prepared to work shifts provided he could have every weekend free! In the end 30 people were called for interview, of whom 20 actually arrived and two were found suitable for employment. When I left Broxbourne some three years later those two were still employed and I found out very much later that they had both gained promotion.

As we desperately needed to fill a vacancy for a typist we placed a notice to this effect in the entrance to Broxbourne station. We received only one application and called Mrs Norma Perkins for an interview, which proved to be the only occasion when I felt that the applicant was interviewing me! Mrs Perkins had full shorthand and typing qualifications and responded heartily to the administration assistant's invitation to question us, probing deeply into such matters as the entitlement to free travel for her and her children. We subsequently wrote offering her employment and gained a very reliable and helpful member of the organisation. I later found out why Mrs Perkins had been so interested in the travel facilities – apparently she had calculated that she could save £1,600 a year if she and the children used them to the full!

Maintaining a full passenger service when there was a high level of vacancies relied heavily on co-operation from the staff. Even when staff were willing to work overtime and change shifts to cover vacancies, there were still times when it was not possible to cover last-minute cancellations. I was in the supervisor's office on Broxbourne station one morning when advice was received that a semi-fast service from Hertford East to Liverpool Street had been cancelled. This service was scheduled to follow a Cambridge to Liverpool Street train and was used by passengers wishing to arrive in London by 09.00 hours. Knowing that the Cambridge service was due I asked the signalman to stop the train at Broxbourne. This was done and the passengers were soon on their way and appeared highly delighted. Less so was the Divisional Operating Manager who telephoned later to say that inter-divisional expresses could only be stopped on the authority of Headquarters Control at York. If similar circumstances arose in the future I was

to advise Divisional Control who would contact York. I pointed out that there was not always time for such a convoluted procedure, but was left in no doubt as to the official view! On the few subsequent occasions when we stopped express trains the signalmen proved very co-operative in experiencing 'temporary signalling difficulties' to justify the train being stopped!

One afternoon the train service to Hertford East was replaced by buses due to a derailment. Some went direct to Hertford East while others served the intermediate stations. As all my senior staff were tied up with duties associated with the derailment I was desperately short of someone at Broxbourne to see that passengers were directed to the right bus. Into the breach stepped Norma Perkins, doing the job admirably and telling me at the end of the day how much she had enjoyed it.

Maintaining discipline in an area where staff shortages were a major problem was not the easiest of subjects as one always knew that if someone was dismissed there would be great difficulty in filling the resultant vacancy. I did not let this influence my decisions, but was surprised at the number of times dismissals arose through the discovery of discrepancies in ticket office accounts. One such resulted from a clerk 'borrowing' £300 for a few days to pay a gas bill, while another was re-dating and re-selling tickets issued for journeys between London Fields and Lower Edmonton. There were two other more serious cases, one resulting in two members of staff being sent to prison, and the other in a clerk being subject to a substantial fine and costs.

In the first case two members of staff in Broxbourne ticket office found a way of producing season tickets without a debit being shown on the machine. The enquiry into this case went on for many months and the British Transport Police and railway auditors were never able to quantify exactly how many tickets had been produced fraudulently. Customers in possession of the illegal tickets were interviewed, one saying that she had been sold her ticket by the Area Manager, who drove a Rover 3500. Fortunately for me and unfortunately for the defendants the Area Manager did not have such a car, but the senior

A photograph taken during my period as Area Manager at Broxbourne; I am wearing my 'Great Eastern' tie.
British Railways

clerk used one for his journey to and from work. The case was initially dealt with by the local magistrates, but was then listed for hearing at St Albans Crown Court when the defendants elected to be tried by a jury. I had never previously been to a court, but as the first prosecution witness I was now to spend some eight days there. I found the trial very interesting, the representatives of both defendants putting a lot of effort into trying to blame the other party. Also interesting was the fact that the police were able to discount evidence given by the manufacturers that a special tool was required to open their machine. At the end of the trial both defendants were found guilty and sentenced to 12 months and 15 months in prison respectively.

The second incident only came to light because one of the relief traffic assistants, Andrew Wilby, grew inquisitive when carrying out a routine audit at Cheshunt ticket office. Having examined the accounts, Andrew decided to compare the record of car parking ticket issues with the actual vehicles

in the car park. He immediately found a major discrepancy. On hearing of the matter I asked both Andrew and the clerk involved to come to my office where I confronted the latter with the facts. I was then amazed to be offered £500 to overlook the matter, but this was clearly an admission of guilt and I had no alternative but to arrange a full investigation by the British Transport Police. The outcome was the clerk appearing in court and being found guilty of a number of offences, dismissal from BR service following.

One other disciplinary case is worth mentioning, if only to illustrate the unpredictability of some events. It concerns a driver at Hertford East whose attendance and timekeeping record was very poor. The matter was dealt with through the internal disciplinary procedure but, somewhat unusually, the staff representatives expressed their concern at the effect of this driver's actions on other drivers at the depot. His continual absences meant that others had to work overtime to maintain the service. Eventually the driver at the centre of this matter was dismissed and, to my amazement, his colleagues went on strike because they felt he had been dealt with too harshly!

Wherever I worked on BR I found unusual practices, and the Broxbourne area was no exception. Wormley signal box, situated between Broxbourne and Cheshunt, controlled main-line signals, signals controlling entry to the loops and a level crossing. The latter was the only level crossing that I ever came across where responsibility for opening and closing the gates was left with the road user – all the signalman had to do was to release the locking mechanism. Not only did this method of operation seem curious to me, but it also caused some public irritation when the signalman had to remind crossing users to close the gates after them. This signal box was also involved in the strange disappearance of a signalman!

Mandatory out-of-hours visits were made to all signal boxes and level crossings every two months. Some strange things were found on some of these visits. One evening Cyril Harris, a traffic assistant based at Broxbourne, paid a visit to Wormley signal box and found that

The first signalwoman in St Margarets signal box, 1978. *British Railways*

the signalman had provided himself with a female companion and a substantial stock of canned beer. Cyril, a qualified signalman himself, immediately suspended the signalman from duty and told him to report to the Area Manager first thing the following morning. Meantime, Cyril took over the box himself and set about arranging the provision of a relief signalman. A report of the Wormley incident was awaiting me when I arrived at Broxbourne the next morning. I expected to see the suspended signalman but he failed to turn up. In fact we never saw him again, and despite numerous enquiries we never did manage to establish where he had gone. When I left Broxbourne his wages were still awaiting collection.

On another of these signal box visits Adrian Milne, a traffic assistant based a Tottenham Hale, found a woman asleep in Northumberland Park Crossing signal box. When he questioned the crossing keeper he learned that the woman was his wife and that she did not like being left at home by herself at night!

I always took my share of these visits and although I never experienced anything out of the ordinary in the inspections themselves I did once have an unusual experience while driving home afterwards. After visiting a number of boxes I had left Ware at about 01.00 and was driving along the A414 near Hatfield when I noticed the headlights of

another car in my mirror. As the vehicle overtook me I noticed that it was a police car, which then indicated that I should stop. A policeman came to my car and wanted to know who I was and what I was doing at that late hour. I explained and produced my driving licence, but he still seemed less than satisfied and asked if I could prove my story. Only when I told him that my signature would be found in the train register of each of the boxes I had visited was I allowed to continue on my journey. I never found out why I was stopped, but I suspect that something unusual was afoot that night.

Derailments in the Broxbourne area were never a major problem, but a couple of incidents stand out in my mind. In the first the driver of an EMU passed a signal at danger at Broxbourne and finished his journey with the leading coach on top of the buffer stops. A photograph in a national newspaper showed the unit surrounded by cows grazing contentedly in the field. In the second incident a wagon was derailed and damaged in a private siding belonging to the local scrap metal dealer. The wagon was re-railed, then left in the siding to await repair by C&W staff. When they arrived they could find no sign of the wagon and we had to assume that it had gone the way of many another vehicle in the dealer's yard! Scrap metal merchants had something of a reputation for cutting up first and asking questions afterwards.

Track maintenance was the responsibility of the Civil Engineering department whose staff regularly inspected all lines, while other staff were expected to look out for possible problem areas in the course of their normal duties. One day a driver working a service to Liverpool Street and doing just this noticed a broken rail on the down line at Cheshunt Junction. He stopped his train and placed a Track Circuit Operating Clip on the line to feign the presence of a train and thus keep the signals at danger, before advising the signalman of what had happened. As a result of his vigilance he received a monetary award for this prompt action, which could have prevented a serious accident. Another driver also received a monetary award after he noticed that a buffer was missing from a wagon on a Freightliner train that had been recessed at Broxbourne to allow a passenger train to pass.

Prior to my appointment at Broxbourne I had never met a BR Chairman, yet in the space of three years Peter Parker visited the area on three occasions. I found him to be a man deeply committed to the industry and very ready to talk to members of the staff.

Although the staff appraisal scheme had been in operation on BR for many years, it was only when I went to Broxbourne that I was called for an interview under the scheme, in 1978. Part of the discussion was devoted to promotional prospects and it was suggested that I should think in terms of moving to Regional or BRB Headquarters. Like many others, this was something I had been trying to avoid for years because I enjoyed being actively involved in current operational activity. While at Broxbourne I had applied and been interviewed for several senior Area Manager's positions, but, heeding the advice I had been given, I now began to broaden the range of my applications.

In a way I would be sorry to leave Broxbourne for it had a marvellous group of

I look on as Divisional Manager Maurice Holmes congratulates Hertford East driver Ian Harvey on his award for vigilance in spotting a missing wagon buffer. *British Railways*

staff working in something of a family atmosphere, and always prepared to help one another if at all possible. But life moves on and in the latter part of 1978 I applied for two vacancies at BRB headquarters.

One afternoon, a little while later, I was in my office when there was a telephone call asking why I had not turned up for an interview at the Board headquarters at Marylebone. My simple reply was that I had not been advised of it, so another was arranged for the following day. Brian Scobey took the interview and quizzed me on my knowledge of the railway system. It must have proved adequate for a few week later I heard that I had been appointed as an Operations Assistant at the Board and would start my new job on 12 February 1979.

10
'THE KREMLIN' AND INTERNATIONAL MATTERS

Monday 12 February 1979 was my first day at BRB headquarters at 222 Marylebone Road. Commonly called 'The Kremlin', this building retained many features from its past, no real attempt having been made to disguise its origins at the turn of the century as the Hotel Great Central, owned by Frederick Hotels Ltd but serving the newly opened Marylebone station. The building itself was almost square with two main entrances, one in Marylebone Road and the other opposite Marylebone station, to which it was linked by a covered walkway. Individual offices were located on either side of a corridor that ran around the building on each floor. Most of the staff were located in small offices that were the original hotel bedrooms, although in a few instances walls had been removed to enable sections of staff whose work was inter-related to be in the same room.

Most of the offices were quite small and I remember that my first office, Room 246, was about 7 feet wide by 12 feet long, with one window that gave a view over the courtyard to the offices on the other side of the building. Toilets were provided on all floors, but here again memories of a past presence were perpetuated by the signs on the doors of the male toilets, which read either 'Officers' or 'Gentlemen'. Baths were still available in some of the former and the building's ceilings and fireplaces also bore witness to an earlier era.

Catering facilities were excellent, with an office trolley service morning and afternoon and a cafeteria providing self-service meals and snacks. Waitress-served meals were provided in a mess for junior officers in management ranges 4 and 5 and in a senior officers' mess for those in higher grades. My grade entitled me to became a member of the former and obtain a three-course meal with a

'The Kremlin' – BRB headquarters at 222 Marylebone Road – in its original guise as the Hotel Great Central.

free glass of wine and coffee available each day. In the light of the emphasis placed on the subject of drinking on duty, especially nowadays, it was surprising that, until 1982, the Board regime was so easy-going, many senior officers having their own office supply of alcohol. It was not unusual for drinks to be offered at a meeting, and some senior staff made a habit of getting together for a drink on Friday afternoons. The catering arrangements also covered facilities for entertaining guests and for providing buffet meals at meetings.

On my first morning my immediate chief, Freight Operations Officer Brian Scobey, introduced me to my new colleagues. In my section of the Operations Department I was responsible for general operating matters, the efficient utilisation of all wagons, including those used for international traffic, and for other non-passenger-carrying stock. Each of these sections was under the control of a manager who reported to me.

I also had a short meeting with Chief Operations Manager Bill Bradshaw, whom I had known since my Reading days. He impressed upon me the need to ensure that my stay at the Board was not too long and suggested that I should consider applying for Divisional Operating Managers' positions after about 18 months. I did not know it at the time, but most of these positions were soon to be eliminated.

After absorbing the responsibilities of my new position I soon realised that, although the whole organisation was clearly defined, some issues were not always dealt with in their rightful places, resulting in senior staff not always being aware of what their staff were actually doing. This problem was highlighted when I was searching for some background information on a particular issue and found that it was being dealt with in three places within the freight organisation.

The general section was located on the opposite side of the corridor to my own office and was concerned with general correspondence and arrangements for the movement of 'sensitive' traffics. These included explosives and traffic conveyed on behalf of the Bank of England. The latter was moved in containers on a small fleet of special vehicles, the only ones not embraced in TOPS (Total Operations Processing System), with the result that their movements were very difficult to monitor. We tried frequently to persuade the users to allow the vehicles to be included on TOPS but without success.

Control and distribution of freight wagons and non-passenger-carrying coaching stock was dealt with in three separate offices. The Central Wagon Authority (CWA) in Room 201 under Frank A'herne (who unfortunately died a short time after retiring) was responsible for the allocation of freight wagons to meet customer requirements. This was the largest part of my section of the overall organisation, with staff coverage provided from 07.00 on Monday mornings to 14.00 on Saturdays. While the Operations Department was responsible for wagon distribution, the actual size of the fleet was determined by the Chief Freight Manager's people.

The ferry section was responsible for the efficient use of all railway wagons on international journeys, together with the compilation of accounts for wagon and sheet hire charges. This section was located on the third floor adjacent to the office responsible for the distribution of non-passenger-carrying stock.

Staff in other sections of the Freight Operations Department were responsible for the daily information and statistics provided in the Headquarters Control Office, for data monitoring, wagon design and modifications, preparation of working manuals, train planning and TOPS.

TOPS was a real-time computer service that was progressively introduced throughout the rail network from the early 1970s. At first the system was confined to controlling and monitoring the use of the wagon fleet, but as time progressed coaches, vans, locomotives and multiple units were also included. For the wagon fleet it was necessary to include the physical characteristics of over 300,000 wagons and allocate a five-digit 'Stanox' number to every location where a wagon could be stabled. The physical characteristics included such information as design code, tare weight, carrying capacity, overall length, floor height, door width and height for vans, brake force and maximum speed. As each area of the network was brought on line, a physical check was made at the same time, with the number and location of each wagon reported to the central computer. In addition, details of the current status of each wagon, ie loaded or empty, and its destination, had to be reported. If loaded, details had to be given of the commodity being carried, its weight and whether specific operating restrictions had to be applied.

During my very first afternoon I found myself the most senior person in the department and was called in this capacity to see the Board member for operations. After I had explained who I was, I learned that this senior gentleman was not satisfied with data supplied to him as a brief for a meeting on the following day. Apparently it was at variance with data supplied by the Chief Freight Manager's staff and I was given strict instructions to find the correct information and pass it to my superior for him to present by 09.00 the following morning. After a lot of trouble I eventually found out who had produced our contribution and was rather pleased when several checks proved it free of errors.

Having spent most of my railway life in positions where I was directly involved in train operation, I was quite apprehensive of a new position that seemed likely to confine me to general office work. At home after my first day I told my wife of my doubts and my reluctance to spend long at BRB headquarters and lose touch with the true world of railways. This same problem affected many people at headquarters, but in my case two new and unexpected responsibilities were to make the job the most interesting and rewarding of my career. It was amazing how the situation was to change from apprehension to wholehearted involvement in things that previously I never knew existed.

On the Wednesday of my first week at the BRB Brian Scobey came into my office and asked me if I understood French. Thinking he wanted a letter translated, I replied that I had learned French at school, had visited France several times and could converse in French in

fairly simple terms. His next remark astounded me – he wanted me to represent BR at a meeting in Paris in May at the headquarters of the Union Internationale de Chemin de Fer (UIC). He went on to say that the agenda would arrive shortly and that I should then get on with the job of obtaining what information I needed for the meeting. No mention was made of how I should respond to specific issues, so I assumed that I would have full backing for any decision I made. Over 14 years this proved to be the case, and no decision I took was ever questioned.

When I went home that evening I was able to paint a very different picture of my position, and asked my wife if she would like to come to Paris with me. Things were certainly looking up, and for the next 14 years, until I retired in 1993, I represented BR at dozens of international meetings within the UIC and with Interfrigo.

Although not directly involved with the Headquarters Control Office, I found it very useful to make a daily visit to peruse the log and examine locomotive availability figures. It kept me in touch with what was happening on the rail network and resulted in me being called upon from time to time to cover vacancies there.

During my second week at headquarters the East Coast Main Line was closed between Berwick and Dunbar when part of the roof collapsed in Penmanshiel Tunnel. In the wake of this incident, while discussions were taking place on the final solution, arrangements had to be made to divert some services via Carlisle and to provide special services between Newcastle and Berwick and between Dunbar and Edinburgh. Because of the additional work resulting from these changes and from the need to amend the TOPS tagging system for freight wagons, I was asked to cover an additional night shift in the Control office. Once again I felt that I was directly involved with railway operations. After many meetings it was finally agreed that Penmanshiel Tunnel would remain closed and the main line diverted around it.

The UIC had been created to harmonise the working arrangements and the exchange of information between railways. For many years BR staff had only attended meetings of UIC committees when specific issues likely to affect them were due for discussion. However, in 1979, when discussions began on the proposed Channel Tunnel, it was realised that even though we were already involved with international services on the train ferries between Dover and Dunkirk and Harwich and Zeebrugge, our involvement would increase considerably when the tunnel was opened. The decision was then taken that we needed to be more involved in the workings of the UIC committees. These dealt with issues submitted by the member railways that required clarification, amendment or new regulations. Disputes between railways that could not be resolved by ordinary liaison could also be submitted for the agenda of the appropriate committee at its next meeting.

Agenda items came under one of two categories, those where the committee could make a decision and others where it would make a recommendation for approval by the parent committee. Decisions in the first category could be published in the appropriate publication relatively quickly, but those requiring approval often took quite a long time. My new responsibilities related to three basic UIC publications, 'The Reciprocal Use of Wagons in International Traffic', 'Loading Regulations for Freight Traffic', and UIC leaflets.

These leaflets were used to circulate information on decisions made by individual railways or a small group that were not acceptable to all. They were divided into sections and covered a variety of issues such as traction units, passenger services, civil engineering, signalling, telecommunications, information technology and travel arrangements for staff attending international meetings. Each leaflet had an individual number and a suffix letter, 'I' indicating that the contents were for information, 'R' that they were recommendatory, and 'O' that they were obligatory (although in some cases mandatory requirements might appear other than in the 'O' leaflets). My main

Typical examples of international wagons.

A Belgian four-wheeled, low-sided wagon with a load of timber.

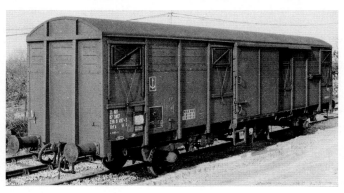

A two-axle SNCF van with sliding door access.

involvement was with leaflets concerned with the operation of freight services – their speeds, formations, braking requirements and technical data on wagons.

I was only involved with committees dealing with freight issues, other appropriate BR representatives attending the other committees. Most of the committees met only once a year, so deferment of items to a subsequent meeting was quite a serious matter, although it did, of course, mean a continuing workload for the committee! Although the committee representatives were fairly senior men, I was surprised how many of them lacked

A two-axle SNCF open wagon with its load secured by straps.

A privately owned bogie flat wagon for long and heavy loads.

A Belgian van with a roller-shutter roof.

precise information about their own railways and were thus unable to make final decisions without delaying the matter under discussion to a later meeting. I can also recall one instance where one delegate agreed a decision, then had to say at the next meeting that his railway would not accept it.

My initial meeting was at the Freight Ad Hoc Committee, whose members were concerned with most aspects of international freight train operations. Operating and technical staff attended the meetings as both subjects were dealt with by one committee, the agenda being divided into operating, technical and joint issues so that delegates could concentrate on their own particular specialisations.

Originally the train ferry service between Dover and Dunkirk took some 3½ hours, but when new facilities were built at Dunkirk West the journey time was reduced to just over 2 hours. The journey across the North Sea was much longer and usually lasted for about 8 hours. Due to tidal conditions at Dover the train ferry vessels had to enter a closed dock, resulting in a turn-round time of some 2 hours. However, at Harwich a floating link span enabled a considerably reduced turn-round.

When I first became involved with international freight working in 1979 there were six daily train ferry services in both directions between Dover and Dunkirk. These were operated by two ships, the *St Eloi* and *St Germaine*, owned by a French company, ALA, but operated by BR and French railways (SNCF) jointly. Each ship could convey 24 standard 40-foot wagons or their equivalent length. If either was unavailable, services could be operated by the *Chartres*, *Vortigern* or *Anderida*, although the latter had a greatly reduced capacity.

Four train ferry ships, owned by BR but operated jointly by BR and the Belgian railways (SNCB), were provided for the service from Harwich, and each of these, the *Norfolk*, *Suffolk*, *Essex* and *Cambridgeshire*, had the same capacity as those operating from Dover. In 1984 discussion began on a proposal to introduce three new vessels on the Harwich-Zeebrugge services, capable of carrying the equivalent of 100 40-foot wagons. The marketing staff had carried out numerous surveys and were confident that sufficient traffic was available to justify this increased capacity. Ultimately one new ship, with only some 50 per cent of the capacity of the proposed vessels, was introduced. Consideration was also being given at this time to the replacement of the ships on the Dover-Dunkirk services, and this was achieved when the *Nor de Pas de Calais* was introduced.

The train ferry services existed principally for freight traffic, wagons being propelled on to the ships prior to the sea crossing, then drawn off at the destination. The Dover-Dunkirk-Dover service was different and unique in that space was reserved on one service in each direction for the conveyance of the 'Night Ferry' sleeping cars, which worked between London, Paris and Brussels. Having used this service on many occasions when travelling to meetings in Paris and Brussels I was sorry when it was withdrawn in 1980. Its great attraction was the sleeping car facility between three major European capitals, London, Paris and Brussels, with an arrival time around 09.00.

All wagons conveyed on train ferry services had to be fitted with securing brackets, which enabled them to be secured to the deck of the ship during the journey by means of adjustable chains. Safety on the sea crossing was of paramount importance, but I do recall one occasion when the crew of the *Anderida*, looking for a quick turn-round at Dunkirk, released the securing equipment before the ships had tied up at the berth. Unfortunately the handbrakes on the wagons had not been applied and some wagons began to move towards the stern of the ship. As luck would have it the leading wagon was a bogie vehicle and the runaway movement was halted when the leading bogie went over the stern of the ship and the wagon ground to a halt on its underframe.

When TOPS was introduced in the mid-1970s approximately 25,000 internationally registered wagons were included in the 'wagon' file as being available for the conveyance of freight traffic on the train ferry services. This figure came down drastically with the subsequent withdrawal of many of them.

Wagons registered in Europe and BR wagons suitable for international services were identified by a 12-digit number, the third and fourth digits identifying the registering railway. Although the BR track gauge was the same as most European railways, there was a considerable difference in the wagon profiles. Most of the European-registered wagons were at least 300mm wider and up to 600mm higher than those used on BR. To identify internationally registered wagons that were permitted to travel on BR an 'anchor' sign was placed on both sides. Wagons involved in transits to Spain and Portugal had to be capable of accepting wheelsets that could operate both on the standard gauge and on the wider gauge that existed in those countries. Most of these international wagons were owned by European railways, BR having only about 400. A small number were owned by private companies.

The largest part of the railway-owned fleet was made up of wagons registered in France, West Germany and Italy. Smaller fleets were registered in Austria, Belgium, Czechoslovakia, East Germany, Switzerland and Yugoslavia. Interfrigo, owned by a consortium of railways including BR, and the Spanish company Transfesa owned most of the privately registered wagons, with a few more in the hands of companies in France, West Germany and Italy.

Strict rules were laid down on the use of railway-owned wagons. To compensate the owning railway for its non-availability when a wagon was on an international journey, a series of daily charges were levied on two-axle and bogie vehicles. These charges were payable to the owning railway when any of its wagons were being loaded, discharged or in transit on another railway. The only exemption was if a wagon was undergoing repairs. If a wagon was damaged beyond repair there was an agreed formula for calculating the compensation to be paid to the owner.

Empty wagons had to be sent back to their registering railway over the route that had been used for the loaded journey. Failure to meet this condition involved other charges to compensate the railway that had to move an empty wagon that had not passed over its system in a loaded condition. At the end of each month each participating railway produced a statement, the RIV Account, giving details of credits and debits between itself and the other railways. Although the number of wagons coming into this country was small in comparison with countries like France and West Germany, we paid out over £1.7 million in 1979. This subject clearly needed to be kept under close scrutiny.

In an examination of the accounts I established that there was a significant imbalance between the loaded wagons received on to the BR system and those being loaded here for destinations in Europe.

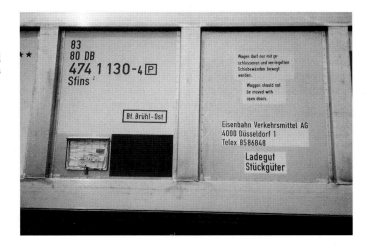

An example of an international wagon number on a German vehicle.

80 DB = registered in Germany
P (boxed) = privately owned
S = flat bogie wagon
f = suitable for traffic with Great
    Britain
i = fitted with mobile cover and
    non-removable ends
n = four axles; highest load limit
    up to 60 tonnes
s = authorised to run under 's'
    conditions with maximum speed
    of 100 kmph (60 mph on BR)

In 1979 just over 9,000 wagons arrived but only 2,800 of them were reloaded. This sort of situation created other problems as instances arose of BR-owned wagons being loaded to destinations in West Germany at the same time as a wagon owned by the West German railways was being returned empty. During subsequent discussions about this with the freight business people, it was decided to withdraw all BR international wagons, which led to a considerable reduction in maintenance costs.

Another factor that caused great concern was highlighted when I established that the average time that a foreign-registered wagon spent on BR was 25 days! Over the course of the next two years considerable effort was directed at resolving this problem to ensure that wagons were discharged as quickly as possible and returned to their registering railways. To monitor the situation regarding delayed wagons a TOPS enquiry was produced that listed all wagons that had been on BR for more than a specified time. It also transpired that many staff at local level were not aware of the costs associated with the detention of these international wagons, or how to differentiate between a railway-owned and a private-owner one. As a result of the various initiatives the average cost to BR was reduced by £1 million and the average time that a wagon spent on the BR system cut by 50 per cent.

When the agenda and associated papers arrived for my first UIC meeting I found that each item on the agenda had a short background note accompanying it. However, this was not really adequate for me as I had not been to previous meetings, and I set about finding out more. No one in my own department had been to a meeting of the Ad Hoc Committee for years, so I tried elsewhere, eventually locating the International Policy Office on Marylebone station. There I obtained valuable information from the staff who also provided copies of the minutes of previous meetings and agreed to translate many of the items concerning technical matters.

Quite a few of the items on the agenda for my first meeting had been discussed on a number of previous occasions, with only minimal progress being made. Three days had been allocated for this meeting starting on a Tuesday and finishing on Thursday afternoon. As air travel was not permitted, the usual practice was to make the outward journey to Paris on the Monday prior to the meeting and return on the Friday. As we had never stayed in Paris before my wife and I decided to go on the Sunday evening's 'Night Ferry' to give us time to find a suitable hotel near the UIC building.

Arriving in Paris on the Monday morning we made our way, after a typical Continental breakfast of croissants and coffee, to the UIC building, which was situated quite close to the Eiffel Tower. We found a very pleasant hotel about 200 metres away and close to a number of restaurants. One of these served a variety of pizzas, all cooked in a wood-burning oven. We went there for a meal one evening to start a habit that lasted through every later visit to Paris, even after my retirement.

On the Tuesday morning I arrived at the UIC headquarters about 15 minutes before the meeting was due to start; a small notice board in the foyer gave the room number. Advance arrangements had been made with the UIC to provide me with an interpreter and, having met Liz Julius, she introduced me to the other delegates as they arrived for the meeting.

Liz originated from the Oxford area so we had many things to talk about as I had worked there for a time. She had been at the UIC for several years and was able to explain the procedures that would be used at the meeting and to introduce me to the other staff working in the 'English' section, many of whom would act as my interpreter at subsequent meetings. It came as a great shock when I heard of the sudden death of Liz some years later.

The BR technical representative at the meeting was Colin May, whom I had first met at the diesel course in Selhurst in 1959, when he was one of the instructors there. It was very noticeable that, in contrast to our single representative for each function, many of the Eastern Bloc countries were represented by two delegates from each. It seemed likely that this was to discourage defection, especially as when one delegate wished to leave a meeting to go to the toilet the other would automatically accompany him! Some of these delegates were staying in the same hotel as my wife and I, but while they would speak to me at the meeting, they ignored me in the hotel.

Having been accustomed on BR to calling people by their first names, it seemed strange at these UIC meetings where the delegates were identified by surname and title of their railway. Under the UIC system each railway was identified by two letters and a two-digit number, which was also the third and fourth digits of the wagon identification number. Examples associated with some of the major European railways are:

SNCF	87 for France
DB	80 for West Germany
DR	50 for East Germany
SNCB	88 for Belgium
NS	84 for Holland
FS	83 for Italy
PKP	51 for Poland
OBB	81 for Austria
RENFE	71 for Spain
DSB	86 for Denmark
NSB	76 for Norway
CFL	82 for Luxembourg
SJ	74 for Sweden
CFF	85 for Switzerland
CP	94 for Portugal
BR	70 for Great Britain
VR	10 for Finland

My first meeting started with the chairman, from Swiss railways, welcoming the delegates to Paris and outlining the programme for the meeting. Discussions on each agenda item were then conducted in French and German with my interpreter translating into English. While simultaneous translation was only used at some meetings, I am sure that it would have much reduced the length of meetings had it been more widely available.

I was not able to contribute much to this first meeting but I quickly realised that other railways were experiencing similar problems to BR. One particular item on the agenda concerned the cleanliness of an Italian wagon. In normal circumstances the organisation responsible for discharging a wagon was also responsible for making sure it was cleaned before return to the owning railway or sent forward for loading. In this particular case the wagon had been loaded with 'white goods' (washing machines) in Italy and sent to a destination on BR. After discharge, as no return load was available, the wagon had been sent back to Italy. While passing through Switzerland it was intercepted by the Swiss railways as they needed a wagon for traffic destined for Italy. This arrangement was perfectly acceptable under the conditions governing the use of wagons in international traffic, but the Swiss claimed that they had to remove a quantity of powder from the wagon before they could re-use it. Through the RIV Account they then claimed the costs of cleaning from BR, but this had been declined.

When this item was discussed the two railways involved, the Swiss and ourselves, were asked to comment on the disputed payment. I could not dispute the Swiss claim that they had had to clean the wagon, but I made the point that since the traffic arriving in Britain could not have produced the powder and it would not have been put in deliberately, the likelihood was that it had been in the wagon when it was originally loaded in Italy. The chairman sagely suggested that the three railways concerned should try and resolve the issue during the midday break. We had a short discussion and decided to share the cleaning costs between the three parties involved.

At the end of the discussion on each agenda item the chairman and secretary were responsible for formulating the conclusions of the discussion and any agreements made. The conclusions were then discussed at the last session, when any arguments that arose usually concerned the translation of what had been said and agreed at the meeting. Very few problems arose with translation from French to English, but translating from French to German was another matter. The conclusions, as amended by this final review, were sent to all participating railways after the meeting. I subsequently found out that in many cases the conclusions had been prepared before the meeting had even taken place!

The derailment at Weaver Junction, a result of insufficient brake-force. *British Railways*

While most of the issues that came before the Ad Hoc Committee did not greatly affect BR, we began to use the committee as a forum for expressing our views on the future of freight train operation.

In 1975 a very serious derailment occurred at Weaver Junction when a train conveying 'dangerous goods' – caustic soda – failed to stop at a red signal due to the high proportion of piped (non-continuously-braked) wagons resulting in inadequate braking power for the weight of the train. It was alleged that the derailment could have been avoided had all the wagons been fitted with the continuous brake. As a result of the inquiry into this derailment BR agreed with the Department of Transport that, from a date to be decided, dangerous goods would only be carried in a wagon fitted with a continuous brake; piped and unfitted wagons would not be acceptable.

To ensure that all Continental railways complied with the new ruling we asked for this item to be listed for discussion at a meeting of the UIC Ad Hoc Committee. There the full circumstances behind the BR decision were explained, but we were politely told that we

could not make unilateral decisions unless the matter was the subject of a governmental directive. European regulations were different and did not match the new BR intention. In many countries the brakes on wagons conveying dangerous goods were isolated altogether if the required brake force could be provided by other wagons on the train, and in Italy the brakes on such wagons were always isolated. When we explained the role of the Department of Transport on behalf of the British Government, the BR decision was accepted with the proviso that a notice thereof should be published in the *London Gazette*.

In 1981 discussions took place at the UIC on proposals to amend the committee structure. As a result separate sections were created to consider individually related issues within a particular railway function. Each committee was given a new title and a numeric identity. Those concerned with operating issues were collectively responsible to the Fourth Committee, and those dealing with technical matters involving traction units, coaches and wagons responded to the Fifth

Committee. Each committee had the appropriate number in its title, those concerned with joint operating and technical matters being given the prefix '45'. So far as I was concerned I became the BR representative on Sub-Committee 4C responsible for freight train operations, and on Sub-Committee 45B, which discussed proposals for new wagons and wagon modifications.

Following changes in the organisation at the Technical Centre at Derby, David Russell, who had been a technical assistant in the Divisional Office at Paddington when I joined the Western Region in December 1963, became my colleague on Sub-Committee 45B. Although initially most meetings had been held on an annual basis, the new committees began meeting twice yearly in an attempt to reduce the time interval between the initial discussions on a proposal and the formulation of an agreed policy. In addition, specialist working groups were created with a remit to examine specific issues and present their views to the main committee.

In 1982 BR began discussion on a proposal to introduce its 'Speedlink' service in the following year. The intention was to apply a minimum speed of 60 mph, with no service guarantee available to wagons that could not meet this standard. At the time of this discussion there was still a large fleet of international wagons whose maximum speed was only 80 kmph, or 50 mph. In the light of this it was decided to raise the matter at the UIC, but at the meeting where our proposals were explained we were again informed that we could not make our own decisions on issues that affected other railways. Once again the London Gazette had to come to our rescue!

Attendance at UIC meetings became a regular feature of my responsibilities and provided the opportunity to visit many European cities, as not all meetings were held in Paris. Most of the discussions related to fairly routine matters, but two particular issues gave me great personal satisfaction. On the first occasion I was asked to give a presentation on the working of the TOPS system to Committee 4C at a meeting in Vienna. The background to this was some 1971 discussions held at the UIC on the

introduction of a form of TOPS, but nothing had ever been agreed.

In my presentation I explained the working of our system together with the cost benefits we had already obtained and our proposals to expand the operation to include such aspects as automatic accountancy between consignors and consignees. I also took the opportunity to explain how we used TOPS for the automatic production of the monthly RIV Account; most of the Continental railways still relied on gathering this information manually. After my presentation arrangements were made for Committee 4C to have a meeting in Derby, which included a visit to Ratcliffe Power Station to see the system in operation.

While most of the committee members could envisage the benefits available from a computer-controlled system used to monitor and optimise wagon utilisation, many others expressed concern at the initial costs and made it quite clear that their railways could not afford the financial outlay.

Interfrigo, with its headquarters in Basle, operated a fleet of temperature-controlled wagons conveying perishable products throughout Europe. Although I was a member of the Interfrigo Operating Committee, I only attended meetings when issues to be discussed were relevant to BR. At one particular meeting a proposal to increase the hire charges for using Interfrigo wagons was listed for discussion and prompted me to spend some time on evaluating its effect. I came to the conclusion that while some railways would have their costs reduced, others, including BR, were going to pay a lot more. I went to the meeting prepared to say that, if the proposal was accepted, BR would no longer be able to accept Interfrigo wagons in future.

The meeting was due to commence on a Tuesday, which necessitated leaving London on the Sunday. However, never having been to Switzerland before, and because my wife was coming with me, we set off for Basle on the Saturday evening service from London. A colleague had given me details of an interesting journey he had made from Basle to Berne and Lucerne and back, including a trip over a rack railway, and I was quite keen to sample this. On arriving in Basle on the

September Sunday morning we deposited our luggage at the Hotel Bristol and set off to explore the city. By lunchtime it was getting quite warm so we spent the afternoon on a river cruise to Rheinfelden. The following day we managed our first journey on a rack railway, my wife later fitting in a trip to Geneva while I was at the meeting.

At the meeting I found other railway representatives who felt the same as we did about the way in which the increased costs had been allocated. Collectively we were able to raise sufficient support to have the proposal rejected in favour of a more equitable distribution of the extra costs.

Railway operational efficiency was regularly discussed at both internal and international meetings, and in 1990 arrangements were made to hold a seminar in Rome on the subject of 'Improving Productivity and Punctuality'. Terry Worrall, the BR Director of Operations, had been invited to present a paper explaining BR's achievements and how they had been obtained. After initial discussion with Terry I undertook the production of an information pack and viewfoils for his presentation. Then, in the week before the seminar and after all the arrangements for Terry's visit to Rome had been completed, he heard that he was required to attend an inquiry into the derailment of a passenger train in Scotland. With some trepidation, especially in view of the very senior representation from the other European railways, I went to Rome in his place and presented the BR position. Fortunately I knew the subject from A to Z having done all the preparation work.

In view of my responsibilities for safe loading on BR and the anticipated increase in international freight traffic when the Channel Tunnel was opened, I decided to look at the International Loading Regulations and compare them with our own. In this area matters where railways differed were discussed at meetings of the Loading Sub-Committee with a view either to accepting the international regulations and including them in the BR Working Manual or trying to persuade Committee 45RIV to amend their own instructions. In most cases we were able

to accommodate the international position in our own domestic controls.

In a few instances, like our use of straps for load securement, the reverse applied. When I proposed the inclusion of a reference to the use of polyester securing straps in the International Loading Regulations it was listed for discussion by Committee 45RIV. At the meeting I explained the BR system, but, after a general discussion, the chairman said that he saw no valid reason for including in the international regulations a procedure that was only used by BR. Clearly some of my colleagues were not aware of what was happening on their own railways, and I had to point out that wagons registered in France and Germany were fitted with the same equipment as that on the BR wagons. After that it was agreed that my proposal would be accepted!

Initially I had only attended meetings of Committee 45RIV as an observer, but in 1987 a BR application for full membership of the committee was accepted. I assumed this responsibility and was also invited to take part in the activities of certain of the working groups examining particular issues. The work on Committee 45RIV gave me a great deal of satisfaction, especially as it was so closely allied to my BR duties. I also took some pleasure in persuading the committee chairman that we might ease formality a little and use first names at the meetings.

To ensure that members of the committee were able to keep up to date on the loading and securing developments on individual railways, meetings were arranged in Austria, France, Holland, Germany and Britain in addition to those in Paris. Most of the committee members spoke at least two languages fluently, but three of us, Jurgen Kotter, Charles Tranchant and myself, were only proficient in our own. At the meetings held away from Paris the host railway provided an interpreter, and in Austria my interpreter was Ulricke Moser. I still recall a comment by Charles Tranchant to the effect that he could not understand why I always got the most attractive interpreters. At heart neither could I!

While the BR loading regulations were contained in a single document, those for the

UIC meetings: interpreters preparing for a meeting in Berlin, and (*right*) Ulricke Moser from Vienna relaxing after a meeting. *Author*

European railways were split into four sections. Sections One, Three and Four contained individual loading regulations, while Section Two gave details on a route basis of the maximum permitted axle loads on individual sections of each of the European railways. On a number of occasions I suggested that the international regulations should be simplified. One major difference between the BR instructions and those applied in Europe was the fact that when we determined a method of loading on a particular wagon it took into account the maximum speed of the wagon, whereas the international instructions were related to the speed of the train on which the wagon was to be conveyed. After I retired discussion began on proposals to update the international regulations and on the formulation of new loading and securing instructions for freight traffic on trains that were to operate at speeds of 100 and 120 kmph (60 and 75 mph).

11
WAGONS, LOADING AND SECURING

The 1980s saw a period of continual change at BRB headquarters, with significant alterations in organisation and individual responsibilities. In 1982 I was asked if I would take over from the Terminal Manager the responsibility for freight terminal operation, including chairmanship of the Loading Sub-Committee and the two sections of the Working Manual for Rail Staff covering wagon loading and labelling. Always keen to extend my experience, I accepted the additional duties. At the same time I found that alterations to the organisational chart had made me responsible to the Operations Officer, Arnold Brown, who was located in the office next to mine. I was also delegated to act as secretary to the Operating Committee,

which was responsible for discussing operational issues and the ratification of decisions taken at the Loading Sub-Committee and Signalling Sub-Committee meetings.

The Loading Sub-Committee consisted of three representatives from the engineering functions, one from the freight business, the Chief Loading Inspector, Wally Curtis, and myself. During the time I was chairman others who attended regularly and made a valuable contribution included Harold Bright, John Gale, David Heath, Paddy McLean, Kevin O'Donoghue, Michael Woodbridge, Rupert Dyer, Ken Hale, Andy Woodcock, Bill Taylor, John Gaunt, Harold Smith, George Brown and Keith Lawson.

Members of the Loading Sub-Committee. Left to right: Arthur Meaby, Harold Bright, Paddy McLean, Wally Curtis, John Gale and myself. *Author's collection*

The committee's remit was to ensure that the safe operation of the railway system was not jeopardised, and to formulate safe loading and securing patterns for all freight traffic, ensuring that the necessary training was given to staff at all levels within the organisation. With my technical background I was able to appreciate the serious problems that could arise if wagons were overloaded.

When Chief Loading Inspector Wally Curtis was due for retirement arrangements were made for his position to be advertised. In due course a number of applications were received and interviews arranged. Following these Bill Taylor, who was the Senior Loading Inspector on the Eastern Region, with over 30 years experience in loading and securing freight traffic, was appointed. In the five years that Bill and I worked together I learned a great deal from him.

As secretary of the Operating Committee I was regularly questioned at meetings about decisions taken by the Loading Sub-Committee. It soon became apparent that the members of the former knew considerably less than members of the latter, so I changed the way in which we operated. The accepted practice was that the Loading Sub-Committee could agree to minor alterations in instructions, with these being published as 'Part Two' minutes. Items requiring endorsement by the Operating Committee were published as 'Part One' minutes. As all of the latter were being accepted I allowed the loading committee to take more decisions and eliminated the need for these 'Part One' minutes. The decision was never questioned and worked perfectly well in practice; I knew that the technical departments were in total agreement.

A few days after assuming my additional responsibilities Arnold Brown handed me a set of drawings for a new international wagon that was being developed by Transfesa. Knowing my technical background, he sought my comments. The proposed design was for a 'De-Bache Vite' bogie wagon with a carrying capacity of 57.5 tonnes of general freight traffic at a maximum speed of 75 mph. This design was new to BR but I had seen wagons of the same type on the Continent and was able to visualise the completed wagon.

John Gaunt checking the securing of a tank of dangerous goods at Dunkirk. *Author*

Detailed examination of the proposals revealed that the wagon had solid bulkheads and was fitted with a concertina-type hood, which could be opened from either end of the wagon to give access to approximately 60 per cent of the overall length – an ideal wagon for the conveyance of palletised traffic. As it was to be used on international journeys involving a sea crossing I was concerned about the safety of the load in rough seas.

At this time BR was in the process of modifying a number of wagons used for the conveyance of steel traffic, and one of the modifications involved replacing the conventional securing chains with winches and polyester straps. The winches were hand-operated with a small tommy-bar and were equipped with a ratchet that ensured that the tension in the strap was maintained. This equipment was much cheaper than chains and a lot easier to use. I therefore spoke to a colleague in the technical department at Derby who was examining the new wagon from a technical standpoint, and we agreed to propose jointly that winches and straps should be fitted. I added a few other minor comments and passed the designs back to the European Rail Traffic Office for transmission to the registering railway.

New wagon design and the modification of

The conveyance of steel slabs only secured by stanchions. *Author*

existing BR wagons were considered by the Traction & Rolling-Stock Committee, which was originally under the chairmanship of Deputy Chief Freight Manager Steve Price, Jim Burnham taking over when he retired. Again as a result of my technical background, clearly serving me in good stead, I was asked to attend a number of meetings of this committee and eventually became its operating department representative. By now it was clear that what I had considered in 1979 to be a rather mundane job had, over three years, become a thoroughly rewarding position with a greatly extended area of responsibility. While the routine work in the office continued, that associated with new wagons and modifications to existing ones was steadily increasing.

At this time the traditional pattern of freight train operation was changing rapidly and with it the profile of the wagon fleet. More block trains were being run and higher-

capacity wagons were being used, some capable of carrying a load of over 60 tonnes. Unfitted and special wagons were being withdrawn, and increasing effort was being put into maximising the loading of the wagons that remained.

In the past wagon capacity had never been fully exploited, but now, as wagon numbers decreased, the Loading Sub-Committee was getting regular requests from the freight business to examine ways of improving loading and securing methods. At the same time the commercial side was working hard to increase the overall tonnage being carried, and many new traffics were on offer, ranging from packaged timber to roof tiles.

In addition to the domestic BR changes, new and modified wagon proposals were being received from private wagon owners. Regular meetings were held with the technical people at Derby and, where necessary, there were visits to the premises of wagon builders to discuss new builds or see wagons in the course of construction or alteration.

To meet international traffic requirements builders were designing bogie wagons with a 20-tonne axle load and a 55-tonne carrying capacity. These wagons were fitted with two or three sliding doors on each side, but after a short period in service some of the first wagons of this design were experiencing problems with the doors becoming detached from their supports. In one particular case the situation became so serious when a door fell off a wagon that we informed the owner that his wagons would no longer be accepted on the BR system unless the problem was resolved. Following discussion with Alan Smith at Derby we agreed a list of modifications required and passed them to the owners of the wagon. A few weeks later the two of us were invited to go to Salzgitter in Western Germany to examine the first wagon modified to our proposals.

At that time it was still BR policy that its staff should travel by rail to meetings in Europe, but the journey to Salzgitter and back by ship and train would have occupied most of the working week. When he heard of our plans the wagon owner offered to purchase air tickets for us, but eventually BR agreed to do

Wagons for conveying timber and roof tiles. *Author*

High-capacity international wagons: (*this page*) a two-axle Transfesa van; a bogie van for carrying coiled steel plate; a bogie van with sliding doors; (*opposite page*) a BR two-axle van with sliding doors; a two-axle van with sliding doors; and a hopper wagon.

Left Studying the door modifications at Salzgitter. *Author's collection*

Opposite Wagons produced by ABRF, Chateaubriant: a Transferry bogie wagon; a wagon for conveying 'swap-bodies'; and a modified Interfrigo wagon.

just this and I made my first ever flight in a BAC 111 jet. At last we were able to prove that air travel could offer a considerable time saving. At the meeting in Salzgitter we found that all our proposed modifications had been adopted and we readily agreed to the modification of the whole wagon fleet.

Following the visit to Salzgitter I was invited to visit Atelier Breton Repairie Ferroviaire (ABRF) at Chateaubriant to examine progress being made with the new De-Bache Vite wagon, which, to emphasise its new design and concept, was called a Transferry wagon. Thirty-five were eventually built and used for a variety of traffics.

ABRF was a family firm, created and owned by Guy Andrivet and employing about 100 people on wagon construction, modification and repairs. Operations began in 1972 and during one of my visits in 1982 the firm celebrated its first ten years in business. A celebration dinner, held in Chateaubriant, was attended by managers and staff from ABRF, the mayor and other dignitaries of the local town, together with senior representatives of SNCF, Francis Billot from Transfesa, and Alan Smith and myself from BR. The meal was typically French with a wide selection of food and wine, which came from barrels rather than bottles, and at the end of the meal I had my first taste of Calvados. Following another meeting with ABRF we had a meal in a local restaurant and I achieved another 'first' – my first taste of

frog's legs, which I found to be very pleasant. Accommodation in Chateaubriant was always arranged by ABRF and on most visits we were accommodated in a local chateau that had been converted into a hotel.

The first Transferry wagon was completed in November 1982. Following normal acceptance procedures it was loaded with palletised bags of china clay and sent to Vitry, where it was put through its acceptance trials. These trials included impact tests, where the wagon was allowed to run down an incline and run into a solid buffer stop, and riding tests on a rolling road where typical track conditions of speed, super-elevation, etc, could be simulated. My technical colleague, Jack Hunt, and I were invited to witness the tests and found them completely satisfactory. I checked the polyester straps securing the load and found that, even after a simulated 8-hour journey at varying speeds, the straps were still tight. In view of my concern at the effect a rough sea crossing could have on the load, it was agreed that the wagon would make a trip on the Dunkirk to Dover train ferry service in January 1983.

I will never forget my visit to Dover to inspect this wagon after its first Channel crossing. The weather conditions were atrocious, with very strong winds and high waves. The train ferry ship arrived at Dover about an hour late and the crew had to make four attempts before they eventually managed to get the vessel into the train ferry berth. Two

of my colleagues from SNCF had accompanied the wagon on its journey and they looked very 'green' when they came off the boat. However, an examination of the load revealed that everything was in perfect order and I authorised the subsequent movement of the wagon to its final destination.

In later years further wagons of a similar De-Bache Vite design were built at Chateaubriant for other private wagon owners for the conveyance of fertiliser. At the time when the Transferry wagons were being built the maximum axle load on many European railways, including SNCF, was 20 tonnes, although on BR we were operating wagons with a 25.5-tonne axle load. Discussions were taking place at the UIC on proposals to increase the European limit to 22.5 tonnes. This was, in fact, introduced before the additional wagons were built, so that the later fleet had a gross weight of 90 tonnes, which made it possible to increase the carrying capacity to around 64 tonnes.

With the trend towards increased palletisation of loads and containerisation, designs were being produced for curtain-sided wagons and those that could be used for the conveyance of 'swap-bodies'. Swap-bodies, unlike containers, do not normally have top-lifting facilities and cannot be stacked. A prototype two-axle wagon for the conveyance of swap-bodies was built at Chateaubriant for Transfesa and, after the completion of satisfactory trials, others followed.

Curtain-sided wagons had been in operation for many years on BR, but following a serious incident at Watford Junction the decision had been taken that any new examples must be fitted with an acceptable form of load restraint equipment. In the Watford incident a curtain-sided wagon, with only chains for load restraint purposes, was being used for the conveyance of motor vehicle components. When a pallet collapsed the contents were not held by the chains and fell from the wagon, derailing a passenger train. This was one of the reasons for requesting the fitting of straps and winches on the Transfesa wagons.

British wagon manufacturers were looking at designs of curtain-sided wagons and the Standard Wagon Company produced a design for the removal of the sides on a normal two-axle wagon and replacement by sliding curtains. This modification was considered necessary as it allowed an increase in the

A BR curtain-sided wagon for conveying steel traffic. *Author*

number of pallets that could be loaded in the wagon. Initially there was concern at the lack of load restraint equipment, but as the wagon was only to be used for carrying palletised boxes containing tins of soup we agreed to carry out trials with the prototype.

The prototype wagon was loaded at Kings Lynn and was accompanied by a loading inspector during its journey on a Speedlink service to Law Junction in Scotland. Regular inspections were carried out on the journey, which passed without incident. After trials lasting four weeks, Alan Smith and I produced a document that was made available to all wagon builders listing the requirements to be incorporated in any design for a curtain-sided wagon. The main point we made was that curtain sides were not acceptable as a satisfactory method of load restraint for general freight traffic, but for wagons that were to be used for specific traffics we were prepared to dispense with the load restraint equipment if trials proved it unnecessary.

When the wagons built for the conveyance of fertiliser were introduced they were fitted with straps and winches, but this proved to be totally inadequate for this type of traffic, and we had to consider other forms of load restraint. The fertiliser, which was in granule form, was contained in bags with a capacity of 500 or 1,000 kilogrammes. To achieve an acceptable payload the bags had to be loaded two tiers high, but while the lower tier was fairly stable, the upper tier was prone to movement during the journey because the lower one tended to act like a balloon filled with water. Various ways of stabilising the load were tried but did not work, the upper bags always tending to lean outwards and infringe the loading gauge.

Eventually the problem was solved by placing a false floor above the lower tier of bags with side restraint for the upper tier to prevent the sideways movement. To eliminate longitudinal movement a 'space invader' method, consisting of two adjustable vertical boards, was introduced. As a result of these trials we were able to obtain a payload of 63.5 tonnes, which produced considerable commercial benefit for this traffic. An initial Continental design for a two-axle, curtain-sided wagon, based on the conversion of a normal wagon, was not accepted when it was found that if the load moved transversely it pushed the curtains outward and created 'out-of-gauge' conditions.

A wagon with a 'false' upper tier and side restraints for carrying fertilisers. *Author*

In 1982 a serious incident occurred at Linslade Tunnel, on the West Coast Main Line, when a prefabricated section of track fell from a wagon and derailed another train. Tragically a driver was killed as a result of the derailment. The track section had been loaded on a bolster wagon with timber packing placed on the bolsters to stabilise the load, which was secured with polyester straps. During the journey the packing had moved, releasing the tension in the straps and allowing the load to move sideways and eventually fall from the wagon.

At the inquiry into the incident it was decided that the cause could be attributed to the fact that the timber used to support the load had not itself been secured to the wagon bolsters. Revised instructions were quickly disseminated making it mandatory for packing to be secured to bolsters. A few weeks later another serious incident was only avoided when a driver saw a rail protruding from the side of a wagon and immediately advised the signalman to stop all trains. In this instance two fishplates had been used in place of a stanchion. Both incidents highlighted the need to ensure that only authorised securing equipment was used and that it was correctly fitted.

When the incident at Linslade was being discussed at an Operating Committee meeting the general view expressed by members was that our training arrangements were seriously inadequate. As a result of the discussion I was directed to arrange a series of Safe Loading Courses. While I would have preferred to have allowed five days for each course, the chairman of the committee, Les Singleton, decided that in view of the seriousness of the situation and the need to train staff as quickly as possible, two courses had to be operated each week.

Never having been involved in arranging training courses before, I talked to other members of the Loading Sub-Committee about the problem and we decided to spend a few days at the Operating Training School at Webb House, Crewe, to decide on the schedule and content of the courses and, most importantly, who should lead them. Eventually we managed to find a group of more than a dozen people who were prepared to help with the courses, and without this help the project would never have got off the ground. Agreement was reached that the course schedule would be based on individual sections of the Green Pages of the Working Manual for Rail Staff.

To make the courses interesting and effective we needed visual aids, and I was gratified to get help in this area from people like Bill Taylor and John Ridley. Bill turned up with a lot of slides showing correct and incorrect methods of securing freight traffic, and John provided viewfoils of individual loading methods.

The courses commenced a few months later with two instructors in charge of each course, and by the time of my retirement over 1,000 members of staff had attended. Our success can be measured by the fact that out of this total only two people felt that the courses were not effective.

When Arnold Brown retired his position was filled by Paul Abbott, but subsequent organisational changes resulted in my position reporting to Paul Grant, the Signalling Officer. However, a further reorganisation transferred me back to the freight operations side under Paul Abbott.

Instructions and regulations for loading and securing freight traffic originated from one of two sources, either from practical experience or from theoretical assessments of a proposed situation followed by service trials. In assessing an individual situation a number of factors have to be considered:

1   the suitability of the wagon for the traffic it is to carry;
2   whether the wagon is permitted in the originating and destination locations and over the planned route between them;
3   the facilities for loading and discharge;
4   the proposed loading and securing arrangements;
5   optimisation of the wagon's capacity; and
6   whether the loaded wagon can be accepted as a normal transit or requires special arrangements.

In addition to ensuring that the carrying capacity of the wagon is not exceeded, care has to be taken to make sure that traffic loaded in open or on flat-bed wagons does not infringe the BR loading gauge, itself a conglomerate of the loading gauges of the many former private railway undertakings.

Originally general loading instructions were contained in a series of 'Green Books', or in local instructions when a particular type of traffic originated from one or two locations only. When the Working Manual for Rail Staff was introduced in the 1970s, Section Two was dedicated to loading instructions that remained applicable. Since this had been first published many changes had been made and additional instructions added following the introduction of new wagons and the acceptance of additional types of traffic. Following the successful introduction of a revised Section Three of the manual, Conveyance of Dangerous Goods, it was decided to examine the other sections.

Instructions relating to freight traffic were contained in three sections of the Working Manual for Rail Staff: labelling instructions were in Section One; loading and conveyance in Section Two; and freight train operation in Section Six. Many instructions in Section Two were also repeated in Section Six.

During preliminary discussions the Loading Sub-Committee agreed to dispense with Section One and transfer current information into Section Two and, where possible, eliminate the duplication of instructions in Sections Two and Six. Following these discussions the committee members spent three days examining each individual instruction to determine whether it was still relevant and deciding how the content and format could be improved. The background to many of the instructions was unknown, and tests were carried out to determine whether they could be relaxed following the introduction of new securing equipment and improved wagon designs. At the end of the three days a basic format had been agreed and the decision taken to provide additional diagrams and pictorial views of wagons to give railway staff a better understanding of the arrangements to be applied to particular loads. It was also agreed to follow the pattern

previously adopted by the Dangerous Goods Committee and include the instructions in a separate document.

The next step was to begin the process of combining the required instructions into a logical sequence and obtaining photographs for the new document. As each new section was completed it was circulated to members of the Loading Sub-Committee and other interested parties to obtain their comments. Eventually, in 1992, a small number of proof copies of the finalised document were printed and circulated with a request for comments. There was general praise for the new format and, especially, the inclusion of photographs, and the printer was given the go ahead once a few minor amendments had been carried out. To allow familiarisation time the new booklet was distributed in January 1993 for adoption in June of that year.

Next, with the accent being on increased payloads, the Loading Sub-Committee began examining various traffics that were operated under special arrangements. One particular flow identified as needing closer examination involved the movement of steel sections in block trains from British Steel at Stoke-on-Trent to Teesside.

Although the wagons used for this traffic were capable of running at 60 mph, for some reason these trains were operated under 'Exceptional Load' arrangements with a speed restriction of 25 mph applied.

As in the case of many other issues examined by the Loading Sub-Committee, we were never able to establish the reasons for this speed restriction. Enquiries on the London Midland Region could not identify any incidents that would have created the need for a speed restriction. All sorts of reasons were considered. Was the speed limitation necessary because many of the sections were considerably longer than the wagon they were carried on and required the provision of 'runners'? But this was discounted as similar loads in the North East were being operated without any speed restriction. Was it due to the fact that many years previously the traffic had been conveyed on wagons that were limited to 25 mph and when alternative wagons were provided no one had thought to use these at their design speed? Was it due to the flexibility inherent in the load sections? Or was it just an 'old Spanish custom'? We could find no satisfactory answer.

Whatever the reason may originally have been, we decided to carry out tests at 60 mph with a loading inspector in attendance. A simple device was fitted to one overhanging steel section to measure its deflection during the journey. At the end of the trial, the Loading Sub-Committee, while noting that considerable deflection of the sections occurred during the journey, was able to agree to the train running under normal conditions as the maximum deflection recorded was within the safety requirement for a minimum clearance of 100mm between overhanging loads and their runners.

While every effort was made to maximise the carrying capacity of wagons, customer requirements sometimes constrained this objective, especially with certain palletised traffic. There were instances of short-wheelbase wagons, with a carrying capacity of 12 tonnes, being used for the conveyance of just one or two pallets, and of even the new generation of long-wheelbase, high-capacity

wagons carrying only three or four pallets. Both wagon types had a maximum speed of 75 mph, and to prevent movement of the pallets during the journey costs of £150 were being incurred for the provision and fitting of timber frames. Obviously if this traffic was to be retained for rail transit something had to be done to reduce the high extra costs associated with securing the load.

Bearing in mind the improved riding characteristics of these particular wagons, it was agreed that trials should be carried out. Two wagons were selected for the trials: a short-wheelbase wagon was loaded with two pallets placed in the centre, and a long-wheelbase wagon was loaded with four pallets, also in the centre. The only restraint provided was to secure the pallets as a single unit with a polyester strap. After successful impact tests the wagons were attached to a variety of Speedlink services and covered a distance of some 1,700 miles under normal train working conditions. The wagons were examined at various locations on their journeys and very slight longitudinal movement of the pallets was noted. At the end they were found to be in almost the same position as that in which they had originally been loaded, enabling us to agree to the elimination of the costs of the timber frames.

Before the introduction of the mass-produced motor car, wheeled and tracked vehicles formed only a small percentage of the freight traffic carried on BR. Then, back in the early 1960s, the LT&S line began to increase its share of the car-carrying business by negotiating first with Ford dealers and later with the Ford Motor Company itself when the

An 'Autic' double-deck car carrier; a 'Comtic' single-deck van carrier; and a 'Procar' 80-car carrier.

latter took over the responsibility for conveying cars from Dagenham to their destinations. Further along this process of increasing the rail carryings of new cars there were discussions between Ford, BR and a private haulier, MAT, leading to the building of a two-tier car-carrying wagon to take the place of the CCT vans and Carflats originally used.

New wagons designed specially for the motor trade and all with metal floors included Autics, which consisted of two double-decked wagons on three axles, designed for the carriage of saloon cars; Comtics, consisting of two wagons on three axles for the conveyance of vans and small lorries; and Cartic-4 units, consisting of four double-decked wagons on five bogies, which could convey a maximum of 28 cars.

The old securing methods had relied on wooden scotches nailed to the wooden wagon floor in front and behind the vehicle tyres. Many of these scotches were damaged during removal and were discarded, but the new wagons gave us the opportunity to use new securing methods, and steel scotches were provided, which, with reasonable care, had an infinite life.

One situation that had not changed for many years was the method of securing military vehicles on Warflat and Warwell wagons. They had always been secured by chains and wooden scotches, but by now the

cost of a replacement chain had risen to well over £100 and the Loading Sub-Committee suggested the use of polyester straps instead. This view was accepted and the appropriate trials arranged.

In the initial stages of the trials, wagons conveying a variety of wheeled or tracked vehicles were subjected to a series of impact tests at a range of speeds up 13 kmph (8 mph). During each test measurements were taken to show the force being exerted on the wagon and the vehicle it was carrying. In addition, the extent of any longitudinal or lateral movement of the load was measured. Although 13 kmph was considered to be the maximum that would apply during normal operations, a misunderstanding during one of the trials resulted in one impact test being carried out at 13 mph instead. As things turned out this gave us an extra result, for examination of both wagon and vehicle showed that neither had suffered from the higher speed.

The second stage of the trials involved the loaded wagons being conveyed on Speedlink services around the system, with examination being carried out at nominated locations. The wagons were being worked under the movement restriction code 'Not to be loose shunted nor must other vehicles be shunted against this vehicle', but, despite this, there was one occasion when three loaded wagons with a combined weight of over 200 tonnes

A metal skeletal wheel scotch.
Author

were shunted into the trial wagon and caused its load to move laterally. When the trials had been completed the Loading Sub-Committee agreed that the revised method of securing could be introduced and the military authorities were advised that they could start taking the chains off and securing vehicles with polyester straps and ratchet tensioners instead.

With the proliferation of modern track relaying methods involving the replacement of older track by continuous welded rail laid on concrete sleepers, the Loading Sub-Committee was asked to consider the methods of transporting this traffic. For many years fixed-formation trains had been used for moving long rails between the production points and the engineering work sites. These trains, like the wagons used for the conveyance of the old 60-foot rails and their wooden sleepers, were only permitted to operate at relatively low speeds. Methods of loading and securing were well established for the older types of wagon.

In their discussions on the new situation the Loading Sub-Committee had taken into account four main factors:

1   proposals being considered for the manufacture of a number of new fixed-formation trains capable of conveying 600-foot rails at a maximum speed of 60 mph;

2   the fact that the Southern Region was already carrying 60-foot rails at 60 mph on 'Parr' wagons;

3   customer requirements – while the 60-foot length was still the standard, other lengths up to 120 feet were being produced;

4   the decision taken by British Steel to concentrate all rail production at Workington.

Normally when new loading instructions were produced they took into account the available facilities at the loading and discharge points. Now, in view of the decision taken by British Steel, the Loading Sub-Committee had an easier task as only one set of loading instructions would be necessary.

Initial trials were carried out with rails loaded on two ordinary wagons with bolsters. Depending on the length of rail to be conveyed, either 'Brill' or 'Mullet' wagons

Trials with the securing of tracked and wheeled military vehicles using polyester straps and ratchet tensioners. *Author*

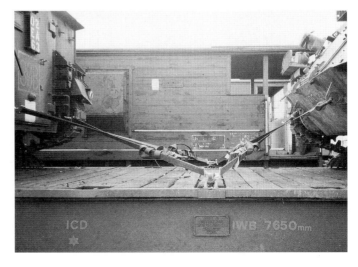

were allocated for the trials. A maximum of four tiers of rails, separated by timber supports, were placed on each pair of wagons and were secured by straps and stanchions positioned close to the load at the end of the wagons. To allow curves to be negotiated the stanchions nearer the centre of the load were not in contact with the rails, which rendered the latter free to slide across the supporting bolsters when the carrying vehicles went round a bend.

At the end of these trials new instructions were issued for the loading and securing of 75, 78, 80 and 120-foot rails. At a later date further trials, including the conveyance of 180-metre rail lengths to the Continent, were undertaken with various wagon combinations. While we had been successful

in our trials with the 180-metre rails, a similar load, using our instructions for its journey from Leoban in Austria to the United Kingdom, became displaced. Resulting from my involvement in our own discussions and trials on the loading and securing methods, I was invited to a meeting with the Austrian railway authorities in Leoban to advise them on our practices. At the end of the meeting I agreed to attend the loading of the trial consignment, but then received no advice of the actual loading date. Instead I was asked to go to Lille, where the displaced load had been discovered, and to advise on its re-adjustment. When I got to France I found that inferior timber had been used to support the rail tiers. During the journey it had become compressed by the weight of the rails above and had

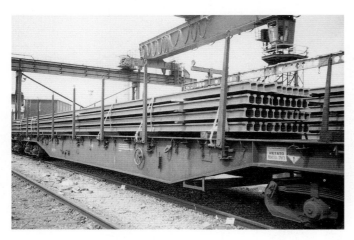

Conveyance of rails: (*left*) 36-metre rails on a bogie bolster, and (*below left*) an en-route view of 300-foot rails, showing the degree of flexibility allowed. *Author*

allowed them to move sideways. The only remedial action that could be taken was to remove the rails and reload the wagons.

When the first of the new fixed-formation trains was completed the Loading Sub-Committee, in conjunction with the project manager John Abbott, produced loading patterns for a range of rail lengths. Rails on these wagons were placed in roller banks with clamps on the central wagon being used to prevent longitudinal movement of the load. On the other wagons the rails were free to move longitudinally within their roller banks, which allowed for buffer compression or coupling extension. On one of the first trials it was noted that rails also tended to move with the application of the train brakes, but a modification of the clamps dealt with this factor.

Two basic methods for conveying concrete sleepers, either by loading them on flat-bed or in open wagons, were considered. While the ends and sides of open wagons provided reasonable load security, the number of sleepers that could be loaded in such vehicles was limited. It was therefore decided to concentrate on the use of bogie flat wagons. As the concrete sleepers were manufactured at a number of points around the country, the Loading Sub-Committee agreed to the regional loading inspectors carrying out their own trials and reporting the results to the committee. At the end of the trials it was considered that the 'Parr' wagon was the most suitable for carrying these sleepers, but, due to their limited numbers, loading and securing instructions were also produced for 'Sturgeon', 'Salmon' and 'Brill' wagons. (The Civil Engineering department had always used extra-traffic wagons for its own loads, and many years ago a decision had been taken to distinguish these by individual names associated with marine fish and mammals. The engineer's stock had these marine names stencilled on the side and they were in regular use for years in telegraph codes. However, such was the depth of the habit that it proved extremely difficult to get Civil Engineering staff to refer to wagons by their three-letter code after the introduction of the TOPS system.)

In 1989 Paul Abbott returned from a meeting with colleagues in Brussels to announce that, in view of the success of the trials we had carried out on the securing of military vehicles on railway wagons, he had 'volunteered' my assistance in trials to be carried out in Europe by a 'committee of experts' from Denmark, France, Germany, Holland, Italy and Luxembourg. The remit for the committee was to produce a document that was acceptable to all railways showing agreed methods of loading and securing for these vehicles. Due to the variety of wagons, securing equipment and vehicles that were to be tested by the committee, meetings were to

The 'Committee of Experts' at Trier in 1990. *Author's collection*

be held in Offenburg, Zwolle, Flensberg, Copenhagen, Trier, Bicester and Florence. When I arrived at the first meeting I found that many of the members of the committee were colleagues who had also attended Committee 45RIV.

It was quite clear from the first meeting, when I presented details of our tests and showed a video of the tests themselves, that apart from the Danish representatives the other members of the committee were not convinced that polyester straps were suitable for securing the vehicles we were to test. Their main attention appeared to be directed towards existing methods of securing by wooden or metal scotches, chains or wire. They did, however, agree to consider any proposals presented by individual members of the committee. Arrangements for the tests were based on the same technical criteria we had used in our BR tests.

In the initial tests at Offenburg existing methods of securing were tested. Most of these proved adequate, but everyone had to admit that a considerable amount of time was consumed in fitting the securing equipment. It was also accepted that many of the wooden scotches would not be suitable for use on a subsequent journey and thus represented a significant cost.

Towards the end of the Offenburg tests the committee chairman indicated that he was prepared to carry out trials with webbing straps. When I saw the ones he was proposing for use I had to voice my concern, for we had tested these straps on BR and found them completely inadequate. They had a breaking strain of only a tonne or thereabouts compared with the 5 tonnes of the polyester straps acceptable on BR. Furthermore on BR polyester straps were used either in conjunction with winches fitted to the wagon or hand-operated ratchet tensioners, and no such equipment existed for the committee's tests. As I expected, when the impact tests were carried out the webbing straps broke. Fortunately the vehicle they had been used on was within a sided wagon so the displacement was limited and there were no serious consequences.

The tests at Trier and Zwolle followed the same pattern as those carried out at Offenburg, but by the time of the Flensberg tests polyester straps, with a breaking strain of up to 10 tonnes, and ratchet tensioners to use with them, were available. I persuaded the chairman to carry out trials with this equipment and these went well, convincing everyone that this method of securing ought to have further serious consideration. The upshot was an agreement that I would arrange tests at Bicester using similar vehicles to those used previously and securing them with BR polyester straps.

In the Bicester tests two loaded wagons were used. One was loaded with tracked vehicles and the other wheeled vehicles. We had only one problem during the tests, and that was when a ratchet tensioner broke, something I had never experienced before. Despite this I was well satisfied with the Bicester tests but the chairman insisted on a re-test. That was also successful, and the results were sent to him. Unfortunately retirement kept me from the final meeting of the 'committee of experts' in Florence, so I did not hear the end of this story.

Containerisation had been developed by the 'Big Four' railway companies in the 1930s to meet increasing road competition and eliminate the time and damage costs of having to transfer traffic between collection or delivery vehicle and rail wagon. The A, B and BD containers were conveyed on special Conflat wagons, to which they were secured by corner chains, and provided a useful and effective freight facility, limited mainly by the restricted size (and thus load) of the containers themselves.

A new era dawned with the introduction of 8ft x 8ft x 10ft long box modules conveyed on purpose-built flat wagons. On the first series of wagons the containers were held in position by air-operated clamps. When all these were engaged a blue lamp was illuminated at the end of the wagon to prove the system. However, problems were encountered and the clamps were replaced by twist-locks, which were fitted to the later build of wagons and provided a simple but effective method of holding containers in position.

Within a few years 20, 30 and 40-foot-long modules were introduced, with widths increased to 8ft 2.5in and heights to 8ft 6in. More recently the height has been increased to 9 feet and, in America, proposals have been considered to increase the length to 48 feet. Before the first 8ft 6in containers could be moved on BR, routes had to be examined to establish where the higher containers could be conveyed without infringing the loading gauge. While containers with a height over 8ft 6ins were not permitted on BR, I can recall an instance when a 9-foot container arrived at Ipswich on a service from Manchester, and a crane driver noticed bricks on the tops of the containers; these proved to have come from Ipswich Tunnel, the old Great Eastern loading gauge being particularly restrictive.

In the late 1980s a prototype container-carrying wagon, with a very low floor, was designed for the carriage of 9-foot-high containers. With the increasing competition between road and rail for the conveyance of freight traffic that could not be accommodated with the existing containerisation facilities, a need was seen for a wagon that could convey road trailers without infringing the existing BR loading gauge. Experience had shown that such a system was feasible in Europe using 'Kangaroo' wagons to convey road trailers over long distances such as the journey between Dunkirk and Modane. Development in this country eventually resulted in the design and production of a prototype 'Piggyback' wagon. The wagon had a centre section that could be swung sideways to allow a road trailer to be backed on. The initial trials, which took place between Melton Mowbray and Cricklewood, went well and, after a few minor modifications, a fleet of these wagons was built.

At the Board there were further changes in departmental responsibilities, with the 'business' sectors taking over more control of their own operational activities. Eventually this led to the final elimination of the headquarters operational organisation that I had joined in 1979. The staff it employed, originally under the control of a Chief Operations Manager and latterly the responsibility of a Director of Operations,

were transferred to other departments. By this time Bill Taylor had retired and his position had been filled by John Gaunt, who had been based in the Regional headquarters at Crewe.

New organisations, with responsibility for technical and operational standards, were created to formulate the standards to be applied to the business organisations. As far as I was concerned my personal responsibilities were not varied to any great extent. I was transferred to the Operational Standards organisation and was still responsible for sections of the Working Manual. However, as a result of these latest changes and others made in the Regional organisations, I lost valuable contacts in Norman Roycroft, Roy Cane, Jerry Loxton, Bob Cochrane and Keith Lawson, who were no longer involved in monitoring accidents or the results of inquiries. I now had to get information from the business managers on incidents that had been reported to the Operations Room, which, in turn, was now the responsibility of the Director, Network SouthEast.

All inquiries into incidents were undertaken by staff from the business sector responsible for the section of line on which the incident occurred. This created situations where an inquiry into an incident involving a freight train could be under the chairmanship of a person who was not involved in freight train operations. One particular incident highlighted the need to have suitably qualified people on the panel for all inquiries.

One evening a report was received that a passenger train had been struck and damaged by a displaced load on a freight train. During the course of the inquiry into the incident it was suggested that the damage to the passenger train had been caused by a concrete sleeper that had moved transversely. While this was quite feasible, the comments made by the guard of the freight train and accepted at the inquiry made me uneasy.

When the guard was questioned about the incident he explained that he had learned of the damage to the passenger train after his own train had been stopped following the incident. He went on to say that when he examined his train he found a concrete sleeper protruding beyond the side of a wagon. When

'Piggyback' wagons, the upper photograph showing the loading method. *Author*

asked what action he had taken, he said that he had pushed the sleeper back into position and had then advised the driver that it was safe to continue the journey. How one man could accomplish this act completely baffled me, so I put my views in a letter to the chairman of the inquiry. As a result I was asked to discuss the complete report with the inquiry team and explain to them the sort of questions that should be asked in any future such cases.

Although I was now a member of the Operational Standards organisation my work with the Loading Sub-Committee, the Working Manual and the international committees still continued, along with other duties that needed attention. All safety publications were now classified as 'standards', requiring an official title and number. In addition, standards had to be written for items to be purchased by the Director of Procurement. Previously these had largely been purchased on the basis of replacing an existing piece of equipment 'like for like'.

In the relatively short period of time before my retirement I was only involved in the provision of two standards, one for a new battery electric tail lamp and the other for a new Section Two of the Working Manual for Rail Staff. Both were completed before I left, but I was surprised to be asked what the position was with the tail lamp standard when I visited the office some time after retirement. This rather confirmed my view that BR was very good at coming up with new ideas but not so good at seeing them through.

In the new organisation I became involved with the British Standards Institute, who were in the process of harmonising standards, initially throughout Europe and ultimately worldwide. As I was fully occupied with my own international railway work, I suggested, and it was agreed, that John Gaunt should represent BR and the BSI at any discussions on the process of harmonisation of standards. Although he attended the initial meetings, a further organisational change at headquarters meant that John was transferred to Railfreight and I had to assume his role at these meetings. Happily, my working links with John continued as he remained the secretary of the Loading Sub-Committee and the work we were doing had much in common. I also knew that I could call on his assistance whenever it was needed.

With retirement approaching I attended only one meeting, in Gothenberg. I expected these meetings to help BR in its aim of having common standards for all activities, but once again there were many voices seeking to retain separate standards for very similar activities. At the meeting I attended a proposal to harmonise security arrangements for maritime safety was being discussed when the delegates from certain Scandinavian countries stated that they wanted two standards, one for 'deep sea' traffic and the other for 'inland seas' such as the Baltic, where conditions were, supposedly, not so severe. Although no final decision was made at that meeting, it was interesting to note that soon afterwards a ship sank in the Baltic Sea in severe weather conditions.

Towards the end of 1992 rumours began to circulate that BR was seeking a major staff reduction in the run-up to rail privatisation; one had it that the cut could be as high as 50 per cent. As further details emerged it became apparent that a reduction of 7,500 in staff was being sought. The aim was to achieve this figure by 20 March 1993 by seeking volunteers to accept voluntary redundancy.

In all the re-organisations that took place in the Operating department at BRB headquarters during my last 14 years with BR, every effort had been made to accommodate people in a position in their substantive grade. However, on certain occasions when this was not possible, staff who were displaced were allocated either to positions in a grade lower than their own or were given special duties. My personal circumstances were that the position I was covering was in a grade lower than my own, although I had never been happy with this grading as most of my work had originally been allocated to people in senior officer grades.

To assist in achieving the required staff reduction it was agreed that a special attempt would be made to find staff who would accept redundancy to allow displaced staff to be accommodated in established positions.

Although guidelines were circulated giving a date of 8 December as the closing date for applications from staff who were prepared to relinquish their position, the attitude adopted by the different departments was not consistent. Some made it clear that no members of their staff would be permitted to leave the service, while others wrote to all their staff seeking volunteers to take redundancy. In the Operating Standards department we heard nothing at all, so three of us wrote to the Director indicating our willingness to go if it meant that displaced staff could have a secure post. At this time, while still enjoying my work, it had taken me away from home such a lot over the previous 14 years that I relished the opportunity of spending more time at home with my wife and family.

The response from our Director gave details of the redundancy payments but made it quite clear that our requests to leave would only be considered if we could find someone to take over our duties. Knowing of several displaced people, I suggested one or two who would be competent to take over my duties after a short period of training, but none of them were considered suitable.

About three weeks before the deadline of 20 March, when I was beginning to accept that I would not be released, John Gaunt rang to say that John Mack, one of the displaced staff of Railfreight Distribution, was interested in my position and would like to talk about it. Arrangements were quickly made for him to come over and see me.

I explained to Paul Abbott what had been arranged, and he agreed to interview John Mack that afternoon. After the interview John was told that he was acceptable, but another two days elapsed while he thought the matter over and while I waited on tenterhooks. At last he accepted my position and arrangements for my redundancy were set in motion. John was released from his current post and spent the last two weeks of my railway career working alongside me.

During the last week I was due to spend three days at a meeting of the UIC, so John was able to come with me and be introduced to my colleagues on Committee 45RIV. I came back from this meeting on the Thursday evening, and spent my last day at work in my office at Paddington.

When I left the office on the Friday it was with very mixed feelings. My career had been interesting, enjoyable and rewarding, and I was happy in the knowledge that by accepting redundancy I was able to provide a post for a younger person, but I would badly miss the colleagues who had meant so much to me over a period of 40 years.

12
REFLECTIONS

During the time that has elapsed since I left BR I have often thought of the people that I met in the course of a career spread over 40 years, and it is very pleasant to be able to keep in contact with many of them, even if it is only through the exchange of letters or cards at Christmas. It is rather sad that many of the colleagues from the early part of my career have died, but their memories will, I trust, live on in my thoughts and in the incidents that I have recalled in the pages of this book. While I have identified many of my colleagues in these pages, there were literally hundreds of others whose names I still recall and who will forever be a reminder of the years I spent with British Railways. To those still working I wish every success.

I thoroughly enjoyed working for BR and could not have wished for a better or more varied career, enabling me as it did to meet so many worthy people, to play a part in a large and important undertaking and to visit so many parts of Europe. My visits to the various towns and cities of Europe gave me the opportunity to witness other railways in operation and the efforts made to improve rail services and their presentation. The most striking transformation was in France with the introduction of the Train à Grande Vitesse (TGV). This is a marvellous example of what can be achieved if, unlike the situation in Britain, the government is prepared to invest large capital sums in trains, facilities and infrastructure.

Through contacts made with other railway colleagues I was able to obtain two trips in the cab of a TGV. On the first trip, from Paris to Lyon at a maximum speed of 260 kmph, I was able to see the extent of the massive engineering work that had been undertaken to eliminate curves and gradients. This trip also gave me the opportunity to study the operation of the new technology associated with automatic train operation at high speeds on lines where there were no signals. The second trip was from Paris to Le Mans, where the maximum speed of 300 kmph was attained once the train was clear of the suburban area.

In Germany and Denmark I was able to travel on the new High Speed Trains of those countries and see how the accommodation for the passengers had been improved. It was also interesting to note that the Continental railways still referred to those travelling by train as passengers, unlike BR where they are 'customers'.

Although there are many highlights in my career, one will always remain special in my memory. On a visit to Innsbruck I was able to make a spectacular trip to the Brenner Pass and to witness there a strange piece of operation that involved locomotive changes at a station where there is a change of electrical voltage. While waiting for a train to return to Innsbruck I saw a train approaching from Italy. Initially I thought it was hauled by a diesel locomotive, as there was no sign of a pantograph. However, when the locomotive passed me I realised that the pantograph had been lowered. After the train had come to a halt an electric shunting locomotive approached and was coupled to the train. The train locomotive was then hauled away towards Innsbruck and once the movement had cleared the points leading back to the station the train locomotive was uncoupled

Travel throughout Europe enabled me to sample the different countries' railways: pictured here are Swiss and Hungarian electric locomotives, and Austrian and French local service multiple units. *Author*

from the shunting locomotive and propelled back to the station. When it got to the other end the pantograph was raised once more and normal working resumed.

While I always made my own arrangements for hotel accommodation when I was attending meetings in Paris, the host railway always made the necessary hotel bookings for meetings in other locations. This system worked very well and only once did it cause some concern. A meeting had been arranged in Berlin in November 1992. I had never been to Berlin before and looked forward to the opportunity of seeing a new city. When the details of the venue for the meeting and the hotel were received they contained directions

on how to get to the latter. On the appointed day I flew in to Tegal Airport, then found my way by bus to a local station for the final leg of the journey to the hotel. Although the Berlin Wall had been demolished earlier it was still possible to see where it had been and it was interesting to see how much progress had already been achieved, including work to improve train services. After changing trains three times I arrived at the station nearest to the Ruchestrasse Hotel, shown in the information sent to me as 45 Ruchestrasse. This is where my problems began.

Making my way to the station exit I found myself in a poorly lit area where four roads met. I knew that my hotel lay along one of these roads but there were no signs to show which was the Ruchestrasse. After searching around for a while I eventually asked two other train passengers for directions and, having got them, proceeded to walk along Ruchestrasse looking for the hotel.

Street lighting here was almost non-existent, but, after passing numerous poorly maintained tenement buildings along one side of the road and the headquarters of the East German Railways and a hospital on the other, I discovered a shop and decided to enquire further. Although my German was poor I managed to find out that the shop was No 73, so I knew I was walking in the right direction. A little further on I came to a sizeable building set back from the road behind a large grassy area. I assumed this was my hotel and began to experience feelings of relief after the long walk through the quite eerie and dismal surroundings. The building offered no entrance at the front but I walked around it and finally found the entrance to the Ruchestrasse Hotel. Presenting myself at reception I was told that I was in Room 310B and was given my keys.

Arriving on the third floor I found a door marked 310 and opened it with one of the keys to find myself in a small lobby with a telephone and a table and chair. Three doors within the lobby led to rooms 310A, 310B and a toilet and bathroom. I used a second key to open the door marked 310B and found myself in a sparsely furnished bedroom with a single bed, a wardrobe and a table and chair.

The room was clean but spartan, and quite unlike any that I had stayed in before. I had seen no restaurants on the walk from the station, so decided to use the one in the hotel. There I enjoyed an excellent meal with one of the other committee members who commented on his own difficulty in finding the hotel and its strange internal layout.

In the morning there was an equally excellent breakfast with the other committee members, following which we all walked to the East German Railway headquarters for the meeting. In daylight the scene seemed even more depressing, with derelict areas abounding and very few cars or buses. All the conversation on the walk to the meeting revolved around our hotel and its strange layout.

When we arrived at the meeting the mystery was resolved by the East German member of the committee. We were told that the building had formerly been the headquarters of the East German secret police. Suspects had been taken and detained there for questioning. The lobbies outside the rooms had formerly housed guards and the hospital I had noted across the road was used for the unfortunates who were injured during questioning.

It was a salutary experience, but somehow typical of the high, and sometimes unusual, interest I had found in a career that had taken me from Salisbury shed to the capitals of Europe.

INDEX